POETRY COMPETITION

₲ReAT MINDS

Your World...Your Future...YOUR WORDS

From Co Antrim Vol II
Edited by Annabel Cook

CU00701768

First published in Great Britain in 2005 by:
Young Writers
Remus House
Coltsfoot Drive
Peterborough
PE2 9JX
Telephone: 01733 890066
Website: www.youngwriters.co.uk

SB ISBN 1 84460 702 X

Foreword

This year, the Young Writers' 'Great Minds' competition proudly presents a showcase of the best poetic talent selected from over 40,000 up-and-coming writers nationwide.

Young Writers was established in 1991 to promote the reading and writing of poetry within schools and to the youth of today. Our books nurture and inspire confidence in the ability of young writers and provide a snapshot of poems written in schools and at home by budding poets of the future.

The thought, effort, imagination and hard work put into each poem impressed us all and the task of selecting poems was a difficult but nevertheless enjoyable experience.

We hope you are as pleased as we are with the final selection and that you and your family continue to be entertained with *Great Minds From Co Antrim Vol II* for many years to come.

Contents

Michael Rutledge (13)   20
Olivia Telford (12)   21
Liam McLoughlin (11)   21
Scott McClenaghan (12)   22
Supreet Jayaprakash (12)   22
Courtney Paxton (12)   23
Stephanie Roy (12)   23
Maureen Reid (12)   24
Rebecca Crawford (12)   24
Amy McClure (11)   25
Amy Adams (11)   25
Laura Dempster (11)   26
James Hyde (11)   26
Natasha Evans (11)   27
Joel Gurney (11)   27
Joshua Gray (11)   28
Sheldon Magowan (12)   28
Jade Mackey (12)   29
Ross Hume (11)   29
David Killen (12)   30
Conor Ferry (11)   30
Kerry Foster (11)   31
Rebecca Gourley (12)   31
Ricky Moffett (12)   32
Mike McFarland (12)   32
Rebecca McGall (11)   33
Jennifer McKay (11)   33
Jonathan Minford (11)   34
Emma McFadden (12)   34
Carrie Ingram (12)   35
Connie McKinstry (11)   35
James Kirkpatrick (13)   36
Laura Hunter (11)   36
Charlotte Lamont (12)   37
Megan Heaney (11)   37
Jimmy Elliott (11)   38
Hannah Hamilton (12)   39
Jake McClay (11)   39
Suzie Ernst (12)   40
Atholl Easton (12)   40
Rebecca Docherty (11)   41
Alison Lawther (11)   41

Victoria Rose (13)	65
Matthew Gleave (12)	65
Lauren Baird (15)	66
Steven Clarke (12)	66
Rachel Ewing (15)	67
Amy Higginson (12)	67
Lauren Thom (13)	68
Grace Shannon (12)	68
Caroline Hull (14)	69
Emma Mullan Osborne (11)	69
Rachel Smith (12)	70
Katie Phair (14)	71
Jody McLoughlin (13)	72
Carrie Lindsay (13)	72
Ben Tisdale (14)	73
Susie Elliott (12)	73
Alexander Arrell (11)	74
Sarah Jane Kennedy (14)	74
Andrew Patterson (11)	75
Geoffrey Campbell (12)	75
Catherine Lucas (14)	76
Gemma Currie (12)	76
Victoria Burke (14)	77
Claire McCartney (13)	77
Jamie-Lee Culbert (16)	78
Gayle Allen (14)	79
Heather Clark (14)	80
Ellie Cameron (12)	80
Chris Molyneaux (13)	81
Laura White (13)	82
Jane Playfair (14)	82
Rachel Walker (12)	83
Rachel Steele (13)	83

Cambridge House Grammar School

Claire Williamson (13)	84
Shelley Malcolmson (12)	84
Natasha McClintock (12)	85
Rachel McBrinn (13)	85
Luke Murphy (12)	85
Aaron Bailie (12)	86

Lois Neely (13)	86
David McMaster (13)	86
Kirstie Bruce (11)	87
William Knox (13)	87
Adrian Hamilton (12)	87
Philip Simpson (13)	88
James McConnell (14)	88
Nicola Lorrimer (13)	88
Rosalind Rowe (13)	89
Carole Duncan (12)	90
Philip Gordon (12)	90
Jordan Cumberland (12)	90
Jason Gault (12)	91
Karen Munn (12)	91
Steve Caldwell (12)	91
Daniel Cummings (14)	92
Laura Rankin (12)	92
Katie Crooks (14)	93
Amy Patterson (12)	93
Victoria Lowry (12)	94
Leeann Gaston (12)	94
Sarah Johnston (12)	95
Rikki Gordon (12)	95
Joanne Fleck (14)	96
Lesley Wilson (15)	96
Melissa Campbell (11)	97
Jessica Boal (12)	97
David Cameron (15)	98
James Moore (11)	98
Joanna Reid (12)	99
Emma Rose (12)	99
Chloe Dalzell (11)	100
Jonathan Small (14)	100
Rachel Allen (14)	101
Michael Armstrong (11)	101
Glenn McGivern (14)	102
Zachariah Deane (11)	102
Ben Houston (13)	103
Lauren Hannan (11)	103
Nikki Tweed (14)	104
Samantha Campbell (15)	104
Amy Lester (13)	105

Carrickfergus College

Parkhall College

Samuel Clark (12)	159
Jodie Taylor (12)	160
Laura Foster (13)	160
Symone Cullen (12)	161
Chris Adamson (12)	161
Nadine Brownlee (12)	162
Robert Clyde (13)	162
Rodger McLaughlin (12)	163
Ashleigh Thorne (13)	163
Matthew McKenna (12)	164
Gary Hume (13)	164
Jodie-Lee Gould (13)	165
Simon Mellon (12)	165
Chantelle Waite (13)	166
Adam Boyd (12)	167
Victoria Walker (12)	168
Kayleigh Melville (12)	168
Aaron Mitchell (13)	169
Shauna Jones (12)	169
Victoria Clements (13)	170
Leanne Adams (13)	170
Christina Maher (13)	171
Lauren Scott (13)	171
Aaron McLean (13)	172
Stuart Mitchell (13)	172
Chris Mowbray (12)	173
Amy Gibson (13)	174
David Pritchard (12)	174
Louise Rooney (13)	175
Naomi Whann (12)	175
Rachel Stewart (13)	176
Adam Jackson (13)	176
Matthew McCauley (13)	177
Stephen Elkin (13)	177
Heather Cosby (12)	178
Laura Mairs (13)	179

The Wallace High School

Sarah Curry (13)	179
Caroline Hynds (16)	180

Nicky Parks (17)	181
Lyndsay Creswell (12)	181
Emma Davidson (12)	182
Andrew Cummings (12)	183
Callum Curry (13)	184
Caroline Davis (12)	184
Caroline Ferguson (12)	185
Gareth Graham (11)	185
Christopher Cousins (12)	186
Matthew Dugan (13)	186
Bethany Downey (12)	187
Julie-Ann Metcalfe (12)	188
Rebekah Dumican (11)	188
Andrew Gilmore (13)	189
Clark Gibb (11)	189
Jed Friskney (11)	190
Chloe Harris (11)	190
Mark Dobbin (12)	191
Michael Christie (12)	191
Jonathan Crean (12)	192
Kathryn Farley (13)	192
Grace Timmons (12)	193
Daryl Corbett (11)	193
Gareth Campbell (12)	194
Rachel Hynds (11)	194
Adam Ewart (12)	195
Rachael Donaldson (13)	195
Jade Drury (13)	196
Leah Hammond (11)	196
Nathan Dickson (12)	197
Stewart Evans (11)	197
Kathryn Dowse (12)	198
Jamie Clements (13)	199
Pamela McClure (11)	200
Jonathan Dunn (13)	200
Sukie McFarland (11)	201
Naomi Fleming (11)	201
Devon Crossley (12)	202
Sarah Geddis (12)	202
Laura Donaldson (12)	203
Jonathan Grattan (11)	204
Emily Gardner (12)	205

The Poems

Roller Coaster

I stood and stared at the monstrous track
It was like a snake twisting and turning
And at some parts it was like a rake.

I looked at the coaster and was frightened
It looked like a dragon with little bars
That grabbed the person and locked themselves.

The roller coaster sped off at great speeds
I felt a hundred needs
Going through my body at amazing speeds
The coaster went to great heights
And there were many sights.

The coaster went through many loops
Which reminded me of corkscrews
The coaster came to an abrupt stop
And everyone got off green-faced.

Alistair Steele (12)
Antrim Grammar School

The Rainforest

It's Mother Nature's wild home,
It's full of exotic plants.
This is a place where animals roam,
There's anything from snakes to ants.

It's got such brilliant waterfalls,
They run so wild and free,
This place has no boundaries or walls,
This place is where we'd love to be.

This really is a sight to see
But we should really leave it alone
This place is a beautiful rainforest
And it's Mother Nature's home.

Walter Todd (12)
Antrim Grammar School

Trampoline

I love the space that I have
On my trampoline,
There's room everywhere
To bounce and jump and be seen.

It is really bouncy,
It throws you high in the air,
Watch out for an aeroplane,
It's right above your hair.

It is very enjoyable,
Something to do in your spare time,
Everyone wants one,
The fun only costs a dime.

The tricks are really fab,
Loads of them to do,
The best is doing somersaults,
My friends enjoy it too.

Timothy Woolsey (11)
Antrim Grammar School

Chocolate

Chocolate, oh chocolate,
What a wonderful thing,
It is as relaxing as hearing birds sing.
I'd eat it all day,
I'd eat it all night,
It is a world of sugar,
Chocolate is such a delight.
Chocolate, oh chocolate,
What a wonderful thing,
It is as relaxing as hearing birds sing.

Debbie Quigley (11)
Antrim Grammar School

Timmy's Babysitter

Timmy was a little boy
Just about two or three
He was as sweet as sugar
In your cup of tea.

His mum worked as a nurse
His dad was a doctor too
So Timmy was landed with an awful person
His babysitter, Lily-Sue.

Her glasses were like milk bottles
She had a cheesy grin
She made Timmy massage her feet
While she took a swig of gin.

'She is awful!'
That's what Timmy would say
She was a lion in her cave
And Timmy was her prey.

When Timmy's mum was having a baby
Lily-Sue said, 'No way!
I'm not minding two babies
So then she went away.

Leah Smyth (12)
Antrim Grammar School

Chips

Chips are lovely when they are crispy,
Chips are like hovercrafts that hover
Across the plate, appetizing your taste buds.
Ooh! What crispy chips.

I love the way they are like Easter eggs,
Because when you eat them they melt
Into your mouth, giving you a relaxed effect.
Ooh! What crispy chips.

Adam Turton (12)
Antrim Grammar School

Saturday Morning

Alarm goes off at 7 o'clock,
I open my eye and look at the clock.
Then it suddenly hits me -
It's football today.

Whatever the weather,
Rain, shine or snow,
I know that today,
I'll feel a wonderful glow.

With shin pads and boots all packed in my bag,
I'm off to play the best game in the land.
We've arrived at the venue,
Determined to win.

When the final whistle comes,
We walk off the pitch happy and loud,
Because we know we've done
Ourselves proud.

Ryan Shaw (13)
Antrim Grammar School

The Sea

The sea is a lion,
As it roars and crashes against the rocks.
The sea smells of chips,
Like a restaurant on the seafront.

The sea is full of fish
And popular with foreigners
Because of the beach,
It's then even noisier.

When no one's around,
The beach is quiet,
But you can still hear the sea,
As it crashes against the rocks.

Simon Wallace (11)
Antrim Grammar School

My Cat, Fred

My cat, Fred,
Loves to be fed.
He's got his own bed,
But he sleeps in mine.
I like that just fine.
He's a stripy little cat
And his belly's really fat.
He sits on my knee,
While I watch TV.
He annoys me when I'm writing,
The end of my pen must be exciting.
So my homework's not so neat,
Because his little feet
Have been standing on the sheets
Of work I have to do,
For teachers just like you.
But Fred just wants to play,
If he got his own way.
He's my cat and he's called Fred.

Lee Scott (12)
Antrim Grammar School

Spiders!

Spider, spider, in my hair,
I squeal, I moan, I cry!
I will not move,
I wouldn't dare!
Oh why, oh why are you still there?

Though I am bigger than you,
Still I am afraid.
I hate every sight of you,
I hate the way you crawl!
I think it's really awkward, but I don't like you at all!

Rachael Walsh (12)
Antrim Grammar School

My Poem

F ootball crazy, I'm football mad
O ne off the lawn playing football with my dad
O n a Friday and Saturday too
T o prove to a manager just what I can do
B ut he never picks me for the team because I have the flu
A ll a big shambles when we're losing 5-2
L ots and lots of torture, off the pitch too
L oud and silent, the manager's assisting too when we're losing 5-2.

Karl Morris (11)
Antrim Grammar School

Puppies

P retty little faces staring up at you
U nder the table they sit and chew
P ure and small like little angels
P ink, red and blue collars
I love little puppies!
E very time I look at them, I just melt
S ome pedigree, some mongrel.
　　Tall, short, fat or skinny, they're all cute!

Jade Lavery (12)
Antrim Grammar School

Puppies

P retty little green, blue and brown eyes
U nder their floppy ears
P ouncing around the house
P laying little puppy games
I nside and outside
E veryone deserves
S omething special - puppies.

Rachel Ingram (13)
Antrim Grammar School

Harley Davidson

H og for short,
A mazingly fast,
R eally well known,
L ike the king of the bikes,
E veryone should have one,
Y ou would have to have an Electra Glide,

D on't think there is a bike better,
A round 26 years old now, the Electra Glide,
V ery famous and very popular,
I 've always loved Harleys,
D id you know Harley Davidson WLAs were used in WW2?
S o old the company is,
O ver 90 years old,
N ever will die.

Stuart Burns (11)
Antrim Grammar School

The Dangers Of Smoking

We have all seen those little white sticks
People put in their mouths.
Little do we know that these little white sticks
With the ginger hair are cackling.
Why? You ask, because they know they are killing you.
Even with the warnings on the box
They will continue to smoke,
Like a steam engine puffing smoke along the track.
With one puff, they become dragon's smoke
Billowing from their noses.
Their life has been shortened by 10 years
Because of that little white stick.
Twenty years later they start shovelling the dirt.
They have perished now, that little white stick killed them.

Philip Walder (12)
Antrim Grammar School

The Untouchables

Arsenal FC is the best,
They beat Chelsea and all the rest.
Arsene Wenger might be a bit weird,
But his Arsenal squad is still the most feared.

With world class players,
Such as Ljungberg and Reyes,
Thierry Henry and Ashley Cole,
Make the opposition scared out of their soul.

With a season unbeaten,
History was rewritten.
We didn't lose to Chelsea,
Man U or Man City.

Champions don't stay still,
They move grounds at free will.
Highbury was outdated,
But Ashburton Grove is highly rated.

So in their new home,
They'll continue their form,
And bring back loads more silverware
And retain their title, I swear.

Scott Newton (13)
Antrim Grammar School

My Hobby

My favourite hobby is football,
I very nearly scored,
I missed the net and after that
I was really bored.
When we were having our next match
I thought it would be
Our best one yet.
Someone passed the ball to me
And I put it in the back of the net.

Tyler Michael (11)
Antrim Grammar School

My Cat

I have a cat called Willow
Her fur is black and gold,
She snuggles on her pillow
To keep from getting cold.

Her favourite meal is Whiskas
She likes to catch a mouse,
She has great, long, curly whiskers
And thinks she owns the house.

She loves to play with balls of wool
Jumps up when you're not ready,
We sometimes think she acts the fool
She even steals my teddy.

Her coat feels like the softest silk
She cleans it every day,
Her wee pink tongue laps up her milk
In a cute, but noisy way.

When I come home she says hello
Round my legs her tail will curl,
I love my cat called Willow
I wouldn't change her for the world.

Alexandra Stubbs (13)
Antrim Grammar School

I Asked The Little Girl Who Cannot See

I asked the little girl who cannot see,
'What is colour like?'
'Why gold,' said she, 'is like a warm fire and a blanket that will
                                    keep you safe and warm.
Blue is like the cold air of winter and an ice lollipop of summer.
Red feels like a really snuggly bed where you feel nice and warm
And where the sun shines.
Silver feels like snow when it falls and it tastes smooth.
And that is what colour is like.'

Alexandra Boyd (11)
Antrim Grammar School

My First Football Match

I can still remember opening my birthday card
And the football tickets falling out.
And here I am driving to the stadium -
Cars are like jelly beans on both sides of the road.
As I get closer, the crowd starts to grow,
The noise is getting louder.
The excitement is growing inside
I think I might burst!
We are in through the turnstile and taking our seats.
An almighty roar goes up as the players enter the pitch.
I can see the wind tiptoeing through their hair -
I can't believe my eyes as the first goal is scored.
Chants roar round the stadium.
1-0, 1-0
It is so much better leaving the grounds
When your favourite team has won.
As we travelled home
I went through the day in my mind.

Ashleigh Watson (12)
Antrim Grammar School

Little Spider

Little spider in the hall,
Are you hiding on the wall?
Little spider, you scare me late at night,
Please don't jump out and give me a fright!

Little spider, please leave me alone
And the hall is not your home.
Spider, spider, I don't mean to be rude,
But I found you in my food!

Spider, spider, please go away,
Isn't there somewhere else to stay?

Vanessa Brown (11)
Antrim Grammar School

The Teddy Bear

I bought myself a teddy bear,
Which was really for Claire, my niece,
He's brown, soft and cuddly
And wears a purple fleece.

I put him in my cupboard,
Until my birthday came,
I then brought out my teddy bear
And played a little trick game.

'Oh look!' I'd say, 'Libby bought it!'
And hold him high in the air,
'Oh, lovely darling!' Ma would say,
'He's the same one you bought for Claire!'

'Oh, I never noticed!' I would lie,
And run back up the stairs,
I'd look around to find a place,
Ah! Right next to all my bears.

Elspeth Woolsey (13)
Antrim Grammar School

Friends

There are only a few important things
A person needs in life,
Very good friends.
If they're good enough,
You will have them all your life.
A friend is like a pillow
That you land on when you fall,
A friend should help you
Through the worst of situations.
I feel so lucky that I have
Such good . . .
Friends.

Emily Adams (12)
Antrim Grammar School

Poppies

You hear the loud guns firing,
You hear the deafening roars,
You hear the death bells chiming,
You hear countries being slowly torn.
The sounds you hear will bring you thought,
Is this the noise while peace is sought?

You see young bodies slumping,
You see the depression and the pain,
You see both sides crumbling,
You see young men bow with strain.
The things you see may bring you tears,
But among the poppies lie their fears.

We know that soon it must all cease,
We know that soon green grass must grow,
We know it must end, causing peace,
But for how long that will last we do not know.
War may come and war may go,
But poppies in great fields will grow.

Helen Peden (11)
Antrim Grammar School

My Favourite Food

My favourite food is Indian food.
It's as bright and colourful
As a summer's night.
So many different flavours,
Spicy and hot,
They all taste just right.
All the different curries
Are paint on my plate.
Yes, my favourite food is Indian food,
So colourful and bright.

Matthew Murray (12)
Antrim Grammar School

I'm Thankful

I'm thankful for my PS2
Without it, don't know what I'd do
I sit for hours to complete a game
Though dinner's ready and Mum calls my name.

I'm thankful for my mobile phone
I spend so much, we'll need a loan
I leave my phone on through the night
No one calls then, but they might . . .

I'm thankful for my mountain bike
I used to have a silly trike
I use my bike to get around
The trike, to Jamie handed down.

I'm thankful for my little sis
She wrecks my room, that little Miss
My PS2 and bike and phone
Are hers, she thinks, when I'm not home.

I'm thankful for the life I lead
Can't think of many things I need -
Perhaps a lock upon my door
So sis can't get in anymore.

Aaron Mitchell (13)
Antrim Grammar School

Hallowe'en

Hallowe'en is a scary time of year,
Beware of witches who have no fear.
We go trick or treating dressed up as ghosts,
We get lots of sweets, who has the most?
Dead things rise over the night,
Don't go outside, you might get a fright.
If anything happens, don't say I didn't warn you,
Look out! Look out! Look out behind you!

David Lucas (11)
Antrim Grammar School

Concorde

She used to zoom through the air
So fast that when you looked up
She was not there.
But then there was that one nightmare
And she was placed back on the ground.

She was the queen of all planes,
The one that they all called the main,
Then she went up, up in flames
And she was placed back on the ground.

She came back again,
She flew again,
She was there for all to see,
But was too expensive
And now is back on the ground.

Now she will stay forever,
On the ground in Toulouse
And one in Manchester Airport,
Never to fly again.

Niall McCulloch (11)
Antrim Grammar School

Tennis

A soft swish and a thump,
Make contact and feel a bump,
Feel the shot, it's going in,
Taste victory, you're going to win,
Smell excitement in the crowd,
Hear them now, they're very loud.

Ben Kelly (13)
Antrim Grammar School

School

School? School's OK,
But we have to go nearly every day.
It's OK I guess and say,
But it doesn't matter anyway.

School, school, school's alright,
But homework, homework every night.
I sit and watch as time goes by,
But it goes backwards, I wonder why?

At ten-past three we are free,
To go home and have our tea.
Free of teachers in every way,
Till we go back the next day.

Jessica Weir (13)
Antrim Grammar School

Winter

Mornings are cold, nights are cold,
This really is getting old.
Lost my gloves, hands are freezing,
Very soon I will be sneezing.

Snowball fights all day long,
Little robins singing songs.
It's so cold, my ears are blue,
But oh look, yours are too.

Lucky for Mum, she's in bed nice and snug,
Why couldn't I catch a bug?
Old Jack Frost's been and gone,
But his mischief still lives on.

Scott Morrison (12)
Antrim Grammar School

Chocolate!

I love chocolate very much,
It's my total favourite food.

It comes in different colours
And it all tastes good.

Galaxy and Dairy Milk,
There are lots of different brands.

But of every one, I must say
I'm a very *big* fan.

To not like chocolate,
I think you'd be a fool.

Because you know what I think?
I think *chocolate rules!*

Laura Richmond (12)
Antrim Grammar School

Me, Me, Me

Michelle is my name,
Hockey is my game,
This poem is about me,
As you will see.

Sometimes I'm lonely,
Sometimes I'm sad,
But other times I'm happy
And other times I'm glad.

Whatever I may do,
Whatever I may say,
I'll always be me,
Until the last day.

Michelle Price (12)
Antrim Grammar School

Ducks!

Flipper flapper,
Fluffy quacker,
Noisy chatter,
Toe tapper.

Widdle, waddle,
Big puddle
Splish, splash.

Big feather,
Mrs Heather,
Little feather,
Baby splasher!

In the end,
It's time for bed,
Chicks cuddle to their mother,
Feeling wrapped in a duvet cover!

Caitlin Weston (12)
Antrim Grammar School

Motocross

In motocross you always get muddy,
When you fall, you might even get bloody.
But anyway, everyone wants to win
And on straights, they always have it pinned.

Honda, Yamaha, KTM,
Every one, like a gem.
Gordon Crockard is one of the best,
He gets big air, over a crest.

The adrenalin rush is such a high,
Table-top jumps, where you can touch the sky,
Win or lose, that's the name of the game,
I'll be back next week, for more of the same.

Jamie Fenning (12)
Antrim Grammar School

My Family

Firstly, there's my dad,
He's a bit mad.
He's always tidying
And then I can't find things.
But he's OK,
I love him anyway.

Secondly, there's my mum,
Sometimes she's a bit dumb.
She always me to today,
You'd think my name was Heidi.
But she's OK,
I love her anyway.

Then there's Matt,
Sometimes he's a brat.
He always calls me ugly
And likes to think he's funny.
But he's OK,
I love him anyway.

Finally, there's Adam,
Nearly as wicked as Saddam.
He loves the PlayStation,
Thinks it's a sensation.
But he's OK,
I love him anyway.

Rebecca Simpson (13)
Antrim Grammar School

My Minimoto

Sitting at the starting grid
On my Minimoto,
The marshal raises his green flag
Ready to shout, 'Go!'

My heart is pounding,
My pulse is racing,
I look both left and right
I really want to beat these guys
I will try with all my might.

The engines rev,
The flag goes down
The race has begun
I've got a good lead
Will I keep ahead?
Is it my turn to say I've won?

Halfway around the track
I end up on my back
No damage done!
The race, it goes on
I've been pipped at the post
By the person I hate most.

He punches the air
As he crosses the line,
This wasn't my day
Maybe next time!

Scott Thompson (12)
Antrim Grammar School

The Man That Fell To Earth

As the
Snow
Peacefully
Falls from the sky,
As silent as an owl
And as pure as a dove,
It forms a man with
A button nose
And two coal eyes that
Stare without a blink. The
Man that fell to Earth. He
Stands as ice, with the moon
Reflecting against the frost
Causing him to shimmer
Like pearls and
Gleam like light. He cannot
Move. All he can do is wait, just
Wait until morning, until the
Murdering sun appears to do one
Thing, and only one thing . . . to
Beam down on this man and kill
The existing frost. The man
That fell to Earth.

Alex Pearce (12)
Antrim Grammar School

Eat Your Greens

'Eat your greens,' is all I hear,
They taste so bad, I shed a tear.
Mum and Dad would make me eat,
The dreaded food that smells like feet.
The filthy food's shoved down my throat,
I won't eat everything like a goat.
I sit upstairs and watch TV
And then have nightmares about a pea.

Michael Rutledge (13)
Antrim Grammar School

Moving House

Boxes, bags, clothes and crates,
Saying goodbye to all my mates,
Will we stay in touch? Will we still be friends?
Or have the happy times come to an end?

Moving house is such a chore,
Twenty-five boxes and there's still more -
The new family is due here at three,
It seems strange because they don't know me.

Yet in my old room they will stay,
Where for seven happy years I used to play.
I look around and my house is now bare,
At the empty walls I stand and stare.

But I don't feel sad because my new house is great,
At last my own room to decorate.
I may paint it pink, red, green or blue,
It's so exciting, everything is new.

Two months on and my new house is my home,
Dusty and Dora love the fields to roam
And my old friends, they still call,
Friends forever, after all.

Olivia Telford (12)
Antrim Grammar School

The Sea

The sea is never-ending blue.
How far it goes we do not know.
It is way longer than I knew.
I think it is longer than others think too.
The waves they crash and they bash.
The waves they wind with never-ending twirling.
When they come back to shore they twist once more.
The surfers, they get really high,
But when they are up in the sky,
They think about how much time flies by.

Liam McLoughlin (11)
Antrim Grammar School

Rugby

Oh rugby, rugby, what a brilliant game
The referee usually gets the blame
The attackers run and score a try
The defence makes the other team cry
The scrum half passes the ball like a bullet
As the forwards maul like they've seen a chicken fillet
The out-half kicks it a mile in the sky
While the centers and wingers run past and say, 'Bye'
The winger catches the ball and runs like a cheetah
He dodges and dodges another player
Then the fullback acts like a tiger hunting its prey
The fullback gets ready to take out the winger
Then all of a sudden *bang!*
All that for the winger to feel a lot of pain
Now it's the other team's turn.

Scott McClenaghan (12)
Antrim Grammar School

My Dog

His nose is long and wet,
His ears are very soft,
He will eat almost anything,
You put into his pot.

My dog is well behaved,
Except when he is angry,
He runs around like a maniac,
But comes back when he's hungry.

He sometimes barks at other dogs,
But I know he's only playing,
I wish that he would stay like this,
But my only hope is praying.

Supreet Jayaprakash (12)
Antrim Grammar School

Winter Mornings

Every morning when I wake up,
I hate the thought of getting up
Out of my bed, just as Mum said
And walking off to school.

I run through the rain,
I slide through the snow,
I start to cough, wouldn't you know,
And with the help of the wind's blow,
I start to sneeze and choke.

Further down the way,
I can hear my mum say,
'Put on your scarf and your gloves,
We don't want you to get cold, love.'

I finally reach a warm school
And it feels so great,
Not to be in school,
But to be with my mates!

Courtney Paxton (12)
Antrim Grammar School

My Black And White Cat!

I have a little black and white cat,
He appeared one day on the backdoor mat.
He comes each day, shortly after eight,
After climbing over the garden gate.
He is a very friendly cat,
But eats so much that he is getting rather fat.
He has a very shiny coat
And loves to get his tummy stroked.
He loves to chase birds and the odd mouse
And often brings one back to our house.
Sometimes we wonder where he's from,
But we know each day for a feed he will come.

Stephanie Roy (12)
Antrim Grammar School

Calum

Nothing compares to you,
Not the waves rolling in on a sun-kissed beach,
Or the first thirst, quenched by the juice of summer fruit.

None of these compares to you . . .

Your love is sure pure,
It is sure to stay,
Until my dying day when I am no more.

You may not know
How much you mean to a twelve-year-old girl that
You call 'sister',
That is why, bro
I wrote this poem,
To show you just how much you mean to me.

How you light up my mornings,
When I see you smile,
And of the warmth I feel,
Looking at the frame of Winnie the Pooh,
With us in it in primary number two.

I know you are not the same
As me, our family or friends,
But that thing called 'autism' doesn't mean a thing,
When you have a sister who loves you so.

Maureen Reid (12)
Antrim Grammar School

Sun Sets

As the sun sets behind the hills
Slowly, silently, creeping, crawling
Comes big, wide eyes like saucers
Watching wishfully, crouching low
            When . . .
Pounce! The wolf leaps on its prey
Satisfied, the wolf starts to eat.

Rebecca Crawford (12)
Antrim Grammar School

Autumn

Autumn coming
It's nearly here
Mother Nature says
It's near

It's getting cold
And misty
The leaves are
Getting crunchy

Leaves are twirling
Down
Then found on the
Ground

All the different colours
Yellow, red and brown
All the different colours
Lying on the ground

It's a disappearing
Sun
Then there's rain about
To come.

Amy McClure (11)
Antrim Grammar School

Horses

Horses are my passion,
More than sweets or the latest fashion!
Tall and strong,
With a mane so long
And eyes as black as coal,
Perhaps someday I'll get a horse,
Or even a little foal.

Amy Adams (11)
Antrim Grammar School

My Home

My home is on the Sevenmile Straight,
It's in the country and I think it's great.
I live with my mum and my dad,
And my brother who's not that bad.
My granny also lives there
And she has curly, silver hair.
In my house I have to do chores,
Which include washing dishes and brushing floors.
My pet fish lives in a tank,
Which sits near the kitchen sink.
In a kennel beside the shed,
Is my dog, Mindy's bed.
I love my home and where I live,
It has so much happiness to give.

Laura Dempster (11)
Antrim Grammar School

My School

Antrim Grammar is my school
Neat and tidy is the rule.
Teaching is what I receive
Reaching for goals I believe.
Instructions are given each day
Made for all pupils to obey.

Ganaway was great for all
Running around and having a ball.
Archery was hard as I was small
My new friends stayed in the hall.
Maths and music have begun
Art and history are really fun.
Rugby is the game teaching us to run.

James Hyde (11)
Antrim Grammar School

A Summer Storm

A summer evening is usually bright
With clouds of purple, pink and white
But those clouds quickly went ebony black
Making you doubt if light would ever come back

Then the rain came down with an almighty crash
As if it was a curtain of water
It was so dense, it was so thick
It was like a flood of molten mortar

Suddenly an awful sound
Slapped into my ears
Oh, the thunder, that dreadful wonder
Next would come the heart of my fears

A flash like a scorching white poker, shooting through the sky
Even though it was only light
It seemed as though it pushed the clouds aside
Yes, this was the thing that I always would dread
A summer storm to knock you dead!

Natasha Evans (11)
Antrim Grammar School

Skateboarding

Me and my mate both like to skate
We skate when we are at our prime
And can't keep track of the time
We practise our ollies
Then practise our nollies
Then practise and practise again
Me and my mate both like to skate
And keep going for five hours straight
We tried to BS disaster
Which ended in plaster
All over our elbows and knees.

Joel Gurney (11)
Antrim Grammar School

Football

Football is fun,
Football is great,
Football is my very best mate.

The whistle blows,
I get the ball,
Even though I'm very small.

Past one,
Past two,
Past another four.

I'm in the box,
I'm going to shoot,
Then I get the boot.

The whistle blows,
Ref points to the spot,
What a marvellous shot.

It goes in the goal,
We've won the cup,
Now we're at the pub.

Joshua Gray (11)
Antrim Grammar School

Oh, Tornado!

Oh, tornado, you wrecked our house
You crept upon us like a mouse.
You horrible thing, you made us flee
From our house - we lived there in harmony.
The shelter hid us from your terror
You piece of yucky, yucky weather.

Oh, tornado, the town is wrecked
The one you had to neglect.
Now you're gone, we live in fear
For we did not realise you were so near.

Sheldon Magowan (12)
Antrim Grammar School

Why?

Why do bad things happen
To those who've done no wrong?
Is it so that one day
It will make them strong?

Without this sort of pressure
We wouldn't really see,
The very special people
They have grown to be.

That wonderful kind of person
Different from you and me,
More determined, open-minded
Faced with difficulty.

I hope that one day we will see
Beyond the chair,
Not notice how they differ
And see the real person
Just sitting there.

Jade Mackey (12)
Antrim Grammar School

Ronaldo

He arrived at sunset
Tired and weary
Hungry and cold
Looking for a home

Dad put milk in a bowl
Mum made him a bed
And a scratch board
And I made him a stretchy toy

I called him Ronaldo
But I don't know why
He plays with a cloth fish
And does back flips.

Ross Hume (11)
Antrim Grammar School

Football

I love sports but my favourite one is football
I play it everywhere - fields, gravel and a big sports hall
To me the best team in the world is Liverpool
Gerrard is their captain and I think that he is really cool

I've been playing football since I was a kid
My favourite position has to be centre-mid
When your teammate runs and has the ball
If you want him to pass, you just give him a call

When you have the ball, you feel really class
But soon you get tackled or have to pass
Football, football, I love football
It really is the best sport of all.

David Killen (12)
Antrim Grammar School

At The Carnival

Down at the carnival there's lots of fun,
If you have money you can buy a sausage in a bun.
There's stupid clowns dancing around,
All you can hear is the carnival sound.

Ghost rides and dodgems along with stalls,
The only thing that bothers you at all,
Is that you're too small
To go on the best ride of them all.

But the worst thing of all is if you're afraid of clowns,
Even though how stupid this sounds.
Some people would pay pounds,
Not to see the delightful clowns.

Conor Ferry (11)
Antrim Grammar School

Brothers And Sisters

The story nearly always goes
As brothers and sisters all should know
That they should hug and kiss
It's something you couldn't miss
Like Hansel and Gretel, stories like that
Not punching and kicking on the living room mat
My sister and I fight all the time
Is it that bad?
Is it a crime?

Brothers and sisters should get along
But if you try, it may go wrong
If you are nice and he is bad
You will end up very sad

So try your best
And see what happens now
Or keep fighting
To start a row.

Kerry Foster (11)
Antrim Grammar School

Heatwave

As I sit here
In my dusty jeep
I look out my window
At the lions leap

Their paws sink into the scorching sand
As they prance across the distant land
My vision in the heat may blur
But still I see their golden fur.

The waves look like mist
The sun looks like fire
And at the end of the day
The lions retire.

Rebecca Gourley (12)
Antrim Grammar School

My Car

I have a Volkswagon Golf,
It has big alloy wheels,
It has a boot spoiler,
I always like to oil her.
She's a sixteen hundred,
I like the way she sounds,
It has a CD player with
Two sixteen inch subs.
It has three windscreen wipers
And a loud exhaust,
It has good, grippy tyres
For driving in the snow.
But that's no good because
We'll not be driving slow.
It also has interior lights
And freaky under-glow.
I can't wait until I'm seventeen
To get my first drive,
To cruise the streets of Antrim
And make me look alive!

Ricky Moffett (12)
Antrim Grammar School

Rugby

'Argh!' yelled the forward while getting tackled to the ground,
'Quick!' shouted the flanker. 'The ball must be found.'
'I've got it, I've got it,' called the prop,
'Whatever you do, do not let it drop.'

Down goes the prop with a venomous hit,
'Keep going lads, keep the fire lit.'
In goes the scrum half to set up a ruck,
The forward picks up the ball and ends up in the muck.

Mike McFarland (12)
Antrim Grammar School

I'm Not Her Friend!

It's all her fault, not mine,
She pushed me out of the line
And said that I had lice,
When I was trying to be nice
And when today I said to her,
'Are you okay? You do look poor,'
She turned around and said to me,
'Go away and leave me be.'
She stomped away in such a huff
And wiped her bogies on her cuff.
When I told her to tie her lace,
She slapped me hard across the face.
At lunchtime things didn't get any better,
She sent me such a nasty letter.
It said, 'I'm going to get you,
I'm going to flush your head down the loo.'
I don't know why she was so mean,
She acted like she was the queen.
She didn't even try to share,
Although I guess I did pull her hair!

Rebecca McGall (11)
Antrim Grammar School

Home

Home is where I shelter from rain, sun, sleet or snow,
Home is where I can always go,
Home is where I learn to cook,
Home is where I can read a book.

Home is where I feel all safe,
Home is where I can hide if there is something I don't want to face,
But last of all, one thing I won't forget,
Home is where the heart is!

Jennifer McKay (11)
Antrim Grammar School

As I Lie In Bed On A Cold Winter's Night

As I lie in bed on a winter's night,
With the wind howling outside
And then me, nice and snug in my bed,
I look down and see a little bit of light
Peeking through the hole at the bottom of the door.

Then I stop and think how lucky I am
To have all this.
I think about all the homeless people
And how they're feeling on this cold winter's night.
Then I think about all the animals outside
And what they're like tonight.

Then I close my eyes
And start to sleep
And all of a sudden
I'm in a world far, far away.

Jonathan Minford (11)
Antrim Grammar School

Summer Holidays

Last summer I went to Portrush,
But on the way home we missed the bus.
We were going to go to the zoo,
But then my brother got the flu.

One day we went to visit my aunt,
But then I tripped over her pot plant.
We went and had a picnic in the grass,
But Dad smashed Mum's best glass.

One day Dad crashed his car,
While trying to take us really far.
Next year we're going to Rome,
But I think we should stay at home.

Emma McFadden (12)
Antrim Grammar School

Daddy's Little Girl

Daddy's little girl
Sits upon his knee,
She smiles and she giggles
He sips his cup of tea.

And while she tells him of her day
He sits and silently prays.

He prays that his daughter
Will live a happy and fulfilling life,
He also thanks God
For the beautiful girl
He's been blessed with.

And when the clock strikes nine,
A gentle hug she bears,
With a kiss on the cheek and a twirl and a leap
She rushes up the stairs!

Carrie Ingram (12)
Antrim Grammar School

Fudge

I really can't wait till Saturday,
Something special is happening to me,
I get my new pup, yippee, yippee!
These few weeks have seemed like years
But now the time is drawing near.
The lady selling the pup then said,
'She's yours now,'
So with a wink and a nudge,
Off we went with Fudge.
When sitting on my knee,
This cute little face peered up at me,
As if to say, 'I'm happy as can be!'

Connie McKinstry (11)
Antrim Grammar School

Rugby

You may think you cannot taste rugby,
But that's not the only thing you don't see.
Please, you have to believe me,
There are some tackles you cannot flee.

You can also taste your own blood,
Not to mention all the mud.
You get rugby pads by Rugby Tech,
But what use is that, flipping heck.

The sand burning like fire on your leg,
'No, please, not the muck,' you plead, you beg,
And the coach, who is like an ogre,
Is always there shouting, 'Ruck over!'

And alas, when you do not win,
All the training goes in the bin.

James Kirkpatrick (13)
Antrim Grammar School

Goodbye, Mrs Green

I really wished that you could have stayed,
To help me learn day after day,
You taught me maths and English too,
You told me rhymes to think things through.

Nobody was as good as you,
Being principal all year through.
You kept me safe all day long
And on Friday mornings you taught a new song.

I will be thinking of you day after day,
Hoping and wishing that you could have stayed.
I enjoyed every moment that you were here,
But I think you need a rest after all these years.

Laura Hunter (11)
Antrim Grammar School

The Sunday Roast Dance

I wait with a watering mouth, anticipating my delicious meal.
I stare in awe at the big black stove as my mother scurries about
                              the kitchen in a mad rush,
Trying to keep everything just perfect.
My nose carefully picks up the aroma of each separate dish,
As it dances gracefully in the oven.
It smells:
The fantastic leg of lamb, the centerpiece in the oven,
Basting in its own sizzling juices,
The crisp roast potatoes worshipping the greatness of the
                              main attraction,
The carrots, sprouts and broccoli dancing their great ceremonious
                              dance.
My mother opens the heavy door and the dancers snap
                              their castanets.
They carry their majestic dance to my lonely plate.
It begins to rain as the minty gravy is drizzled over them.
The table is set.
I am licking my lips with my knife and fork in hand.
I start eating.
The dancing stops.
There is silence: then music!
It starts again.
A new parade on my tongue!

Charlotte Lamont (12)
Antrim Grammar School

Holidays!

We stayed in a caravan on our holidays,
We had so much fun.
My little sister Katie, my dad and my mum.
We played on the beach and rolled in the sand,
We went for long walks, Katie holding my hand.
We all had so much fun, but also shed a tear,
Mum says not to worry, we're going back next year!

Megan Heaney (11)
Antrim Grammar School

My Summer Holiday

I spent my summer holiday
In a cottage in Donegal,
Halfway up a mountainside
Far away from it all.

No telephone or videos
No computer or Game Boy,
We watched wild animals and birds and plants
That's how we got our joy.

My daddy took us fishing
To lots of different places,
Cold mountain lakes and sunny beaches
Brought wonder to our faces.

We kept a little tally
Of the species that we caught,
We rated them on 'scrumminess'
On a scale of ten to nought.

The brown trout was delicious
The sea trout simply fab,
We all enjoyed the mackerel
The flounder and the dab.

But the one we scored above the rest
Was gurnard fried in batter,
We ate so much that fortnight
That we all came home much fatter!

Jimmy Elliott (11)
Antrim Grammar School

Swimming With Dolphins

This summer I'm going to Florida
It'll be even better than last year
I'm swimming with dolphins
In the blue water clear

I can't wait to go
It's going to be so much fun
Dolphins performing tricks
Under the beautiful yellow sun

Dolphins are such fun to see
Dancing and splashing with such glee
As a butterfly flitters and flees
Carried along in the warm breeze

Gliding through the water
Like a rubber ring
The dolphins making funny noises
It's almost like they sing

This year I'm going to Florida
And I am really excited
I'm swimming with dolphins
I am truly delighted.

Hannah Hamilton (12)
Antrim Grammar School

War

All the soldiers were shouting, 'Retreat, retreat!'
But I continued down the ruined street.
There were guns blazing and bullets flying,
As I ran on, I saw dead bodies lying.
I climbed up to a machine gun turret, just above the lake,
But little did I know, that was the last move I would ever make.

Jake McClay (11)
Antrim Grammar School

Why Not?

How come lads never let girls play football?
It's my favourite sport.

They always have to make up excuses,
Like we're not tough or too short.

They just *try* to look tough,
When they spit and swear and shout,

And us *girls* are so elegant among the players,
Weaving in and out.

So listen here now girls, if you want to play football, fine,
No need to hear *them* out.

If they want to complain, fine,
Ignore them without a doubt.

But for today, anyway,
We're stuck with them, okay?

But don't forget,
Teamwork's what football is all about.

Suzie Ernst (12)
Antrim Grammar School

Vegetable Soup

In my mum's cooking pot was vegetable soup,
There were all types of vegetables, from A-Z.
The carrots to me were like little logs floating in a lake,
Others like little Titanics.
The potatoes were the biggest of all vegetables in the pot,
They were the kings of the vegetable jungle
And no one could match up to their superior strength
And intellect.
But when I put them into my mouth,
They knew that I was the king of the vegetable jungle.

Atholl Easton (12)
Antrim Grammar School

My New School

At the end of Primary 7,
It was just like Heaven.
We did the same things every day,
I could not wait for new subjects on the way.

It's now early morning when I rise,
I rub the sleep out of my eyes.
As I leave, my mum shouts to me,
'Have you got your bus pass and your key?'

My Ganaway trip was fun,
By the sea, but never sun.
Three days of constant rain,
But making new friends eased that pain.

Now we have settled in,
The real work will begin.
Head in books, learning every rule,
Now I am a pupil at Antrim Grammar School.

Rebecca Docherty (11)
Antrim Grammar School

Food

Hamburgers, chips, baked beans too
All mixed together waiting for you,
We never eat vegetables or fruit for that matter too,
Chocolate is nicer and better for you!
Fries are tasty and full of fat
Designed to make you want more of that.

Lettuce and celery are what you should eat
They say they are tastier than any other treat.
A heart attack is where you will end
If your diet you don't mend.

Alison Lawther (11)
Antrim Grammar School

Gymnastics

I love gymnastics
It's really fantastic
I started when I was eight
And thought it was great
The first thing was floor
That started two hours after four
After that was the bars
Which I found really hard
My favourite is beam
That was really clean
Last is the vault
Where you run, jump and halt
Class ends at eight
Which I really hate
My dream is the Olympics
So that I can high kick
In my floor routines
Or maybe the bars and the beam
Until then my friends
I shall continue to bridge and bend.

Rebecca Edmondson (12)
Antrim Grammar School

Doggies

Always ready to run a mile
Just to see my doggie smile
Great for playing with and having fun
Great for cuddling when the day is done.

Always jumping and running
Never can find time to calm down
Oh! My dog is such good fun
A perfect pet for everyone.

Tia Dawson (11)
Antrim Grammar School

Chocolate

Chocolate is my favourite thing
When I see it, I could sing.
It is lovely, soft and creamy
And it makes me feel dreamy.
Galaxy is my favourite bar
It's the creamiest, dreamiest one by far.
Every Friday I get sweets
And oh! how I love these special treats.
At Easter all those creamy eggs
Make me wobbly on my legs.
And Christmas is the best of all
With selection boxes in the hall,
And tins of lovely chocolate sweets
To give all my family a treat.

Robyn Foster (11)
Antrim Grammar School

Skating

I love skating, it's as fun as can be,
Whizzing down a hill,
My friends and me.

My favourite skater is Kareem Campbell,
When he enters a competition,
Everyone scrambles.

When he does a crazy lip,
He lands it
And doesn't slip.

Then he lands a 360° ollie
And then moves on
To an incredible nollie.

Patrick Lecky (11)
Antrim Grammar School

The Seashore

As I walk along the seashore,
I can taste the salty air,
Running my hand through the waves,
Smooth and ragged, all at once,
As they crash along the shore.

I smell the chips and candyfloss,
From stalls along the beach,
And watch the foam, mingled with blue,
Swirl like marble paints,
Washing all my cares away.

The sea can be angry,
A monster eating the beach,
It can be calm or windy,
A friend to sailors as they fish,
But it's always beautiful.

Rachel Lewis (12)
Antrim Grammar School

A Poem For You And Me

Poems can be funny
Poems can be sad
They can be about a bunny
Or a little bit of money
They could rhyme
In time
Or it could be like a story
About a little boy called Rory
Poems could be about pets
Or little flying jets
Poems can be any size
Any shape at all
Poems are a piece of writing
Which are fun to read and write
Poems are spectacular
So read, read, read.

Hayley Donaldson (11)
Antrim Grammar School

The Storm

The cool breeze blowing in my ears,
I can hear the lightning cracking far off.
Then, it's so close, I could reach out and touch it;
A huge ball of energy.

The lightning strikes and I can taste the almonds in the air.
A metallic smell is hovering just above me.
Suddenly, like a bomb, it explodes
Making the very earth shudder.

Then it disappears into the night.
The static energy crackles like popcorn,
Pricking my ears like tiny, invisible needles.
Silence . . . the storm is over.

Peter Heyburn (12)
Antrim Grammar School

Dreams

In amongst my clouded brain,
Among my thoughts of sun and rain,
Are many exciting scenes,
That come from my daily dreams.

Sometimes at night I wake up and scream,
Because I've had a scary dream.
Sometimes I wake up and cry and cry,
Because I've just seen my family die.

They don't have to be logical,
But sometimes they're magical.
I like to have happy dreams,
Sometimes while the sun still beams.

Sometimes I just float on a cloud
And maybe just float around,
But when I wake up, they're always gone,
When I wake up at the crack of dawn.

Nicola McKee (12)
Antrim Grammar School

The Grandfather Clock

In my grandmother's big old house,
Once stood a grandfather clock.

It stood in a big, empty room,
At the top of the great house by a window.

There is silence in the room,
There is only one sound in the room,
This is the low, gentle ticking.

There is one smell in the room,
This is the strong scent of mahogany,
The mahogany casing that holds the great clock face.

I once put my hand on the great clock face,
It felt like a small heart going thump, thump,
On the palm of my tiny hand.

Samara Grant (12)
Antrim Grammar School

Music

My favourite type of music is pop,
But I also really like hip hop.

Someday I would like to be a pop star
And I hope I will go really far.

My dad likes to listen to jazz,
But I think I'd rather do my maths.

My sister is listening to R 'n' B,
While my mum is drinking a cup of tea.

My friend was in the choir,
But she got thrown out because she can't sing any higher.

My cousin who lives in France,
Really thinks he can dance,
But I said he was bad and now he is really sad,
I think he can only prance.

Amanda Lee (13)
Antrim Grammar School

Sisters

Sisters are annoying,
But also can be fun,
They can be loving
And pretty like the sun.

They might take our things and hide them,
Or give them to a friend,
But we tell them,
'Next time ask and I'll lend.'

Sisters can be company,
When we're lonely or we're sad,
They can help us through,
Good times and bad.

They might hit and kick us
And never mend,
But sisters really are,
Our best friends.

Leone Law (13)
Antrim Grammar School

The Moon

The moon is a football up in the sky,
It is also a giant blueberry pie.
The moon is a target waiting to be shot,
It is also a massive white blood clot.
The moon is an egg laid by a duck,
It is also a shot-put too big to chuck.
The moon is a beacon to guide us all,
It is also a colourful, bouncy ball.
The moon is a place where few have been,
It is also a sight commonly seen.
The moon is a face watching over the Earth,
It sees every death, it sees every birth.

Mark Lewis (12)
Antrim Grammar School

The Peaks

Slowly, I trudge along the peaks of snow,
How old I am I do not know.
Here, the frost wipes memories clear,
Among the snowy peaks.

I feel as if my spirit is sold,
A friend to me would be like gold.
Here, the loneliness leaves you dry,
Among the snowy peaks.

I press onward, heart in hand,
I have to stop, I cannot stand.
My hope is slowly wearing thin,
Among the snowy peaks.

I see shelter, not far away,
I crawl along, my life at bay.
As I approach, I wish I was home,
Among the snowy peaks.

I seem to deny the inevitable end,
I don't have much time left to spend.
Now I realise, this journey was worthless,
Alone, among the snowy peaks.

Andrew McFadden (11)
Antrim Grammar School

The Sun

The sun is an orange beach ball thrown up into the air.
It is a gold coin fallen down a drain from Heaven.
It is a droplet of a mango smoothie .
It is the queen of the stars.
It is as hot as lava.

It is the sun!

Caroline Bingham (11)
Antrim Grammar School

The Tale Of Black Bob

My name is Black Bob,
Piracy is my job,
So with cutlass and pistol,
We set sail from Bristol.

We strike fear in our foe,
Wherever we go,
But the place where we reign,
Is the whole Spanish main.

On board the Black Pig,
We drink rum and jig
And as cannonballs thunder,
We pillage and plunder.

My hearties take pleasure,
In stealing lots of treasure,
As we fill the ship's hold
With silver and gold.

With a parrot and eye patch,
Ladies think I'm a right catch,
But I prefer a good fight,
To an amorous night.

Colin Turk (13)
Antrim Grammar School

The Fog

Sweeping in from across the wide, grey sea,
A huge, blurred mass coming steadily nearer,
Wrapping long, damp fingers around the coast,
Destroying your sight, like a soft, grey blindfold,
Somehow drowning other sounds,
Leaving a calm, mysterious silence.

James Gardiner (13)
Antrim Grammar School

Hardcore Gamer

Gaming on my PlayStation
Cheating at Sim City, rising the population
Playing Tekken Four, fully cleaning house,
Playing Toca Racing, unlocking cat and mouse.

When I buy a new game
I play it, then I name and shame.
I buy a mag called Power Station,
I think it's the best in the nation.

Some games keep me on my heels
Others are as shocking as electric eels.
In some games there are blood and guts
In others there are psychos and nuts.

In Driver 3 there is racing and tooting
Also driving and shooting.

Some complaints from drivers in games -
Why did you ram my car in the sea?
I'm not a scuba diver, I ran over a salesman
And in the road lies his liver.

Come on you granny wagon
I can't stay here all day!
Get off the road you stupid boy,
I don't want to play.

The game selection is wide and vast
I love to win and sometimes I'm last
What the 'ell, I'll give it a blast!
The hardcore gamer.

Daniel McNeill (11)
Antrim Grammar School

Food

Vegetables are yucky,
Especially mushy peas,
Broccoli and cauliflower
Taste like mouldy cheese.

Crisps and chocolate are the best,
They are my favourite food,
If I could eat all the crisps in the world,
I know I definitely would.

I hate fish and spicy things,
They make me want to cry,
If I was forced to eat them,
I would probably die.

Burgers, hot dogs and pizza,
Are tasty in every way,
Junk food from chip shops and sweets from a jar,
Cannot be beaten - no way!

I know tasty foods are not good for my health,
They may not be good for me,
But I'd rather die or be critically ill,
Than have to eat broccoli!

Amy McIlwaine (12)
Antrim Grammar School

Spring

Flowers are smiling
In the sunshine,
Butterflies are playing
In the meadows,
Leaves are shining
In the garden,
Birds are singing
In the trees.
Spring is a blessing from nature and God,
Which attracts me so much to nature and God.

Basil Babu (12)
Antrim Grammar School

New Zealand Rugby

Rugby is a sport which you can't blame
For the riots and people who claim.
When they score,
They rant and roar.
When Joe Rococoko runs and roars,
Tana Umaga drops and scores.
Conversions - Carlos Spencer is your man,
He kicks with a wham.
Rucks and mauls,
Kicks and brawls.
Supporters far and wide,
Players run and stride.
The game is won,
The players are done.
The supporters go home,
Into their room
And boast over the phone.

Andrew Megahy (12)
Antrim Grammar School

Morning's Messenger

In the morning it shows its glory,
Warming the Earth, keeping it glowing.
Slowly emerging from the pits of night,
Shining, smiling, burning bright.

Smoothly it rises, arousing all nature,
Awakening the birds, predicting the weather.
It shines its beauty, tremendous and bold,
The round, burning sun encrusted with gold.

Looking down on us with shimmering splendour,
It glistens, gleams on its beholder.
Daytime has ceased and the sun will die,
Descending softly in the night sky.

Tracy Ceaser (14)
Antrim Grammar School

Blinded By Ignorance

Why is it always
'Under the moon'
Or 'beneath the stars'?
Why not 'above the grass'
Or 'amongst the air'?

Why do we always think
That the world is huge?
What about all the other
Planets out there?
Or what about the sun?
It is really a midget
Compared to other suns,
Not a giant, as we think.

We think we are the best
And made ourselves what we are.
We think we're so high tech.
Haven't you thought
Beneath the surface
We're highly corrupted,
We blow each other up,
Just because of one dictator's views.

Why are we picky
About the truth?
We only want to know it
If it's good.
If it isn't, then forget it,
We don't want to know it.

Can't you see the filthy truth?
Or are you just an ignorant youth?

Harry Cameron (14)
Antrim Grammar School

Spaghetti Bolognese

The mountain so high,
With boulders falling from the sky.

The hot and spicy smells,
Go up through your nostrils
And make your nervous system tingle.

The soft, slimy spaghetti,
Slithers like a snake,
It sticks to the fork and curls up in a ball.

It calls out,
'Eat me,
Eat me.'

When it touches your tongue,
Fireworks go off inside your head.
Your taste buds go wild
And vibrate with satisfaction.
Finally, when swallowed,
The mouth is left empty and wanting more.

Rachel Devine (12)
Antrim Grammar School

Bobbie The Dog

B arks all the time,
O ne of a kind,
B rindle is his colour,
B ouncy as a bubble,
I nstant fun,
E ver causing trouble!

T he size of two daisies,
H is eyes outshine the sun,
E ars as pointy as a fox.

D otty as a dice,
O riginal and divine,
G lad that he's mine!

Genna McGilton (13)
Antrim Grammar School

Christmas Dinner

We have opened our presents,
It's time for lunch,
Soft, chewy roast turkey
And carrots to munch.

As we enter the kitchen,
The aroma of turkey fills the room.
We stop and stare
And do nothing but drool.

The juicy roast turkey,
Gets sliced on a plate,
My tummy is rumbling,
Waiting for bait.

The dinner set out,
Just waiting to be eaten,
My stomach a black hole,
My heart hurriedly beating.

I take my first bite,
It melts like chocolate in my mouth.
My stomach overjoyed,
Singing from north to south.

Sarah Fulton (12)
Antrim Grammar School

Creatures Of The Sea

Deep blue saltwater,
Home to creatures great and small.
Fish, dolphins and great blue whales,
All together in the sea.

Coral, plankton and jellyfish,
Dance like underwater ballerinas.
Sand, salt and open water,
Perfect for a nice summer's day.

Shana Irvine (13)
Antrim Grammar School

The Night Sky

Sleeping beauty
Daylight gone
Moonlight's up
Sunlight's shone
This is why the daylight's gone.

A night in Heaven
Is in cloud number seven
Moonlight's up
Sunlight's shone
This is why the daylight's gone.

Morning is near
There is no fear
Moonlight's up
Sunlight's shone
This is why the daylight's gone.

The sun rises
The moon descends
Daylight's up
Moonlight's shone
This is why the moonlight's gone.

Awoken beauty
Moonlight's shone
Daylight's up
Moonlight's shone
This is why the moonlight's gone.

William Nimmo (11)
Antrim Grammar School

Distant Memory

When I think of you
You're a distant memory,
It's been a while
Since I last saw you.
I dream of you
Night after night
And think of you
Day after day.
Still you're just a
Distant memory.
I cry for you
But you don't hear,
I want to see you
But you're not there.
I find it hard
To think of you,
Because you're just a
Distant memory.
I try to imagine
Your smile,
But it feels like
My heart's on trial.
You feel so far,
Far away right now,
How am I going to cope?
Because you're just a
Distant memory.

Tina Ho (15)
Antrim Grammar School

Rugby

As we start the game,
I can see the other team.
We hear the whistle go,
Then the ball is kicked and off we go.
As the ball flies it's like a kite,
Soaring through the sky,
Then the ball is passed to me,
I can feel it in my hands.
It's like a diamond, but not as rough or tough.
As I am running, I get tackled
And I hit against the ground,
I can taste the grass
That went into my mouth.
Such a horrible taste,
I can smell the soil,
That smells rotten.
As I look up, I see the teams
Driving up above me,
Pushing to one side,
Going the other,
I see the scrum-half
Picking up the ball
And as they all break up,
I get up to continue the best game I know,
Rugby.

Blake Pattison (12)
Antrim Grammar School

Own Goal

A ball going thump, thump, thump.
Hear the team, 'Kick it in now!'
See the goal, it's over there,
Taste anxiety in the air.
Kick the ball and the other team go mad,
That was the wrong goal! Now I'm sad.

Courtney Gilmore (12)
Antrim Grammar School

A Tropical Island

I imagine the sound of the steel drums,
Many people dancing and celebrating,
Wearing shirts as bright as the sun.
Yet when I look around, there is no one here.
There is silence, apart from the tide,
Washing up and down the beach,
The lonely palm trees sway in the gentle breeze.

I can smell spicy foods,
Chillies and spices remind me
Of the sun's intense heat.
I taste tropical fruits,
Lemons, mangos and pineapples,
Their juiciness quenches my thirst.

A tear rolls down my cheek,
I wish people were really here,
Dancing and celebrating.
I search the beach, it's deserted,
There's no one here,
I'm all alone.

Rebecca Grant (13)
Antrim Grammar School

Hallowe'en

'Happy Hallowe'en,' the kids all shout,
It's that time of year when witches are about.
Fireworks go high up into the sky,
The witches are waiting for people to die.
'Don't be afraid,' my friend did say,
But, that was before she flew away!
High in the sky, she flew overhead,
'Look out, Vicki, you'll soon be dead.'
All of a sudden I felt myself shake,
'Come on, Vicki, it's time to wake.'
Oh, I am so glad that I am not dead,
It was only a dream and all in my head!

Victoria Harvey (12)
Antrim Grammar School

It

Black and stormy was this Monday night,
It woke up and took flight,
Down the stairs without a creak,
Through the hallway it did sneak.
The room *It* entered was pitch-black,
More so than any witch's cat.
Still moving here and moving there,
It made no sound with utmost care.
Something *It* was searching, looking, lurching,
Then just as quick as *It* came,
Up the stairs, *It* went back again.
Early next morning, Mum, she pointed,
Cookie jar empty, Dad disappointed.
Then slowly turning around,
It was coming with a bound.
Mum and Dad could really see,
That after all that, *It* was *me!*

Christina Cosby (14)
Antrim Grammar School

Cold Country Mornings

The mornings smell like fresh fruit,
Sweet and calming.
This smell will always be my favourite.

The mornings feel like soft velvet,
Rubbing against my hands.
This feeling will always be my favourite.

The sounds are like birds flying in the sky,
Whistling in my ears.
This sound will always be my favourite.

The sight reminds me of a swan,
Swimming across a lake.
This sight will always be my favourite.

Cold country mornings will always be my favourite.

Lauren Smyth (11)
Antrim Grammar School

Under The Moon

Deep down in your garden in the middle of the night.
There will be magic going on by a pixie or a sprite.
Prancing by the lanterns, playing by the light,
Streams of glitter left behind when they're in flight.

Watch the fairies dancing beneath the gleaming moon,
Sprites seem to move to their own secret tune.
The best time to see the magic dance is in June,
If you have never seen the magic, do so soon.

If you want to see the magic, try not to scare,
Pixies have sharp hearing, so tread with care.
You could try and catch a fairy if you dare,
But if they see you, they will turn you into a bear!

The magic fairies disappear when it turns dawn,
They leave a track behind, like dew on the lawn.
When you wake up, the pixies will have gone,
Although the sprites disappear, the magic lingers on.

Rachael McBride (14)
Antrim Grammar School

War

Leaving our families crying in the street,
Scared for our lives, as we may never again meet.
Herded to the battlefield,
Marched like cattle to the slaughter.

The stench of death can be tasted, mingled with fear.
Carcasses lie on a carpet of red,
Where their life's blood was poured out.

As I look around I can hear
Bombs exploding, as death comes near, near.
Soldiers take their last breath of life,
Praying for this suffering to end.

Gillian Fleming (13)
Antrim Grammar School

Heartbreak

You are my one and my only,
Without you my heart would be lonely.
My love for you is plenty,
If you weren't mine, my heart would be empty.

We are destined to be together
And that's how we will be forever.
With you I can spend hours,
That's because our names are written in the stars.

I can't stand to be apart,
It almost breaks my heart.
You and I are such a perfect match,
When they made you, there wasn't a batch.

You say you need some space,
So, I am trying to keep a brave face.
Bit by bit, part by part,
It's plain to see, you're breaking my heart.

Now you've left me,
You want to be free.
What about what I want?
What about me?

Dar 'Oma McAloon (14)
Antrim Grammar School

The Only Horrible Sound

If I could hear the sound of nails scraping the board,
It would taste like a mouthful of acid,
Drip by drip down my throat.
It would smell like revolting garlic going up my nose,
While I'm tasting the acid.
If I could touch it, it would feel like earwigs
Crawling all over my body,
And if I could see it,
It would look like a never-ending tunnel
Going on and on and on.

Eileen Orr (11)
Antrim Grammar School

Homework Is Great (Not!)

I really don't like homework,
I think it is a real bore,
No matter how hard I try,
I never get a good score.

Why do we have to have homework?
Any sort is bad.
I can't find the answers in my head,
It makes me very mad.

Oh, how I hate to do homework,
It drives me around the bend.
Why are the teachers so mean?
They could just make homework end.

I'm not too fussed on homework,
It's not my favourite thing.
I think I do enough work in school,
Without extra work to bring.

You see, this poem is homework,
It's worse than any test.
I'm struggling to find the last line,
So teachers, *give me a rest!*

Rachael Blair (12)
Antrim Grammar School

Shopping

S hopping, oh shopping, is a delight to some,
H appy, having so much fun,
O pening the door smells like a fresh new day,
P lease Mummy, give me the money to pay,
P lastic bags filled with clothes, CDs and more,
I t's a world of goodies galore,
N ever bored doing this,
G oing shopping, oh what bliss!

Kate Ridley (11)
Antrim Grammar School

A Water Poem

Water is as soft as silk,
When you touch it,
It ripples away in miniature waves so perfectly rounded.
It smells like a brand new car,
It tastes like watery apples
And sounds like a waterfall
Falling over the side of a mountain.
If we didn't have this marvellous thing,
Nothing would be alive -
Not us,
Or animals,
Or plants,
Or trees,
Absolutely nothing.
So think next time you go to use water,
How marvellous it actually is.

Jack Parte (11)
Antrim Grammar School

Shopping!

Shopping has an exciting feel to it, like sweets
Trapped in a tube and they are trying to get out.
It looks like a food court where everything is all packed together.
Oh, how I love to shop, for shoes and clothes and sweets,
Oh, how I love to shop.
It feels like lots of soft teddies wanting to jump into my hands.
When I listen, all I hear is people talking and fussing.
Shopping is like ice skating when you bump into everybody,
It is so packed.
I love the smell, it is like toffees,
Shopping makes me feel free,
Oh, how I love that feeling.

Hannah Young (11)
Antrim Grammar School

What I Like . . .

I like my coffee with sugar and cream,
I like to think, to hope and dream,
I like the colours pink and blue,
I like to think you like me too.

I'd like it if I was never late,
I'd like to be a perfect size eight,
I'd like an 'A' in every test,
I'd like to think I try my best.

I'd like a text from a forgotten friend,
I'd like some things to never end,
I'd like to pass notes all day with my mates,
I'd even like fifty first dates!

I like to read late at night,
I'd like to get a maths question right,
I like when Chris Moyles is on the radio,
I like to watch re-runs of an old TV show.

I like to talk to friends on the Internet,
I'd like to win a million-pound bet,
I like my coffee with sugar and cream,
I like to think, to hope and dream.

Victoria Rose (13)
Antrim Grammar School

My Poem About War

The sun is slowly rising,
I'm fighting for all I'm worth,
I can't forget the suffering,
Of my fellow men at work.
But now it is all over,
The battle has finally finished,
We're packing up and leaving
And waiting to go home.

Matthew Gleave (12)
Antrim Grammar School

Life's Dream

I lie in bed every night thinking of what might be,
All the places I could go and things I could see.
It's always been my life's dream to meet someone like you,
Now finally, after all this time, my life's dream has come true.

You're always there when I'm in despair,
You love me and let me know that you care.
When there was no one else around, you gave me hope,
Now that you're here, I feel I can cope.

I trust you with every deepest secret,
No need to worry, I know you can keep it.
You've helped me overcome my fears,
You very rarely bring me to tears.

I know I'm aggressive, messy and loud,
Being with you makes me so proud.
I've had lots of problems in the past,
Before you came along, I didn't think I would last.

I lie in bed every night thinking of what might be,
All the places I could go and things I could see.
It's always been my life's dream to meet someone like you,
Now finally, after all this time, my life's dream has come true.

Lauren Baird (15)
Antrim Grammar School

Autumn

Autumn is back, it's time to relax,
Until winter is back.
The hedgehogs are hibernating,
Uncle Dave is sound asleep
As I look out the window.
Everything is cold, still and quiet.
Something stirs in the tree as I look up,
I can see a robin looking down at me.

Steven Clarke (12)
Antrim Grammar School

Disastrous Tendencies

Let's bomb some random countries,
Who cares who we kill?
Let's do our best to their country,
Till it's lonely, dead and still.
Let's forget about our conscience,
Push all the guilt behind,
Regain our label 'terrorists',
I'm sure they wouldn't mind.
We'll destroy some lives, make children cry,
Make women scream in fear,
Make sure they can't rebuild their lives,
To no effect we see their tears.
We realise we are evil,
What we do is egotistic,
We'll be irrational, unfair and cruel,
All but realistic.

Rachel Ewing (15)
Antrim Grammar School

Blue

Blue is like the ocean
Blue is like the sky
Blue is what I felt like
When my special goldfish died.

Blue is the pen I'm writing with
My Tipp-Ex mouse too
Blue is my French classwork book
Oh no, this reminds me of school!

Blue is my school uniform
My favourite colour too
Blue is my mum's car
Oh, it's blue, blue, blue!

Amy Higginson (12)
Antrim Grammar School

Shopping

Shopping is great,
Shopping is cool,
If you don't like it,
You're a big, stupid fool.

So much to buy,
So much to choose.
That saucy pink lipgloss,
Or a new pair of shoes?

Get to the till,
To pay for my bling,
I whip out the plastic,
It buys me anything.

On the way home,
Out of the town,
The car's stuffed with bags
And then it breaks down.

It can't handle the weight,
Of my scary obsession.
But it costs a lot,
To be in fashion!

Lauren Thom (13)
Antrim Grammar School

The Patchwork Quilt

The patchwork quilt
God created
Sewn together
Like man had made it
Up in the sky
So high above
All the pieces
Fit like a glove.

Grace Shannon (12)
Antrim Grammar School

The Butterfly

The transition is complete,
It's time to break free
From this cramping coil
That has encompassed me.

Emerging slowly,
I flutter a wing,
I'm king of the insects,
A superior thing.

My robe is of jade,
My throne way up high,
I'm graceful and majestic,
Soaring toward the sky.

All too short is my reign,
Life's gone in a flash,
I return to the earth,
With a thundering crash.

Caroline Hull (14)
Antrim Grammar School

My Favourite Food

My favourite food is chicken curry
Not to be eaten in a hurry
Sausages, burgers, chicken nuggets and chips
These things are great, but go straight to your hips.

Hot dogs, popcorn, kebabs and ice cream
Add up the calories and you're certain to scream!
As you can see, I love all of these foods
Because they all put you in different moods.

All these foods must come second best
Because chicken curry outruns all the rest.

Emma Mullan Osborne (11)
Antrim Grammar School

Sweets

Bitter like fizz
Sweet like honey
Sour or tasteless
They're all very yummy.

Candy buttons
Chocolate towers
Shaped like animals
Or even cars.

All these things
I like to eat
Are the very wonderful
Delicious sweets

Yellow like the sun
Blue like the sky
Green like the grass
And my very own eye

Smells of exotic fruits
And flowers
They're as large as footballs
Or as small as stars

All these things
I like to eat
Are the very wonderful
Delicious sweets.

Rachel Smith (12)
Antrim Grammar School

The Hostess

(This poem is based on Lady Macbeth's thoughts after receiving her husband's letter, which tells of his encounter with three witches)

As my eyes carefully scan
My husband's written thoughts,
Revealing revelations
Of truths we've been taught.

I feel anticipation
Flutter through my soul,
'Dearest partner of greatness',
Ambition, I can't control.

I force him to act
Upon the things they say,
Knowing, hoping, waiting,
Praying for the day.

A crown upon our heads,
Sceptres in our hands,
I start to realise that,
Not all is according to my plan.

He almost lets it slip
The dirty deed that we have done,
I feel the pressure rising,
This fear compares to none.

Now he has struck again
Killing his own best friend,
It seems he's changed forever,
Nothing good can his evil mend.

Katie Phair (14)
Antrim Grammar School

The Ocean

The ocean is a vast plain of non-stop blue,
It is amazing, even if you don't have a clue,
I myself could look forever,
No matter what the weather.

Would you believe that people are afraid of such a big, blue thing?
All it does is make me sing.
As I look from this far-off cliff,
All I feel is pure bliss.

I can never sleep
When I think of a thing so beautiful and deep.
When I look at this beautiful place,
I cannot believe it helps the human race.

When I look at this big, blue thing, I feel so alive,
I still don't believe we need it to survive.
The one person I feel like praising,
Is God for making a place so amazing.

Jody McLoughlin (13)
Antrim Grammar School

Comfort Eating

Arriving home after a bad day at school,
Depressed at the heap of homework to follow.
Throw bags down and head to the kitchen,
Hesitating momentarily at the fruit bowl,
Craving sugar, open snack cupboard.
Thrusting hand into cereal box,
In an instant, it is gone.
Rummaging through the cupboard once again,
Emerging with colossal quantities of biscuits, sweets and nuts.
Temporarily high on sugar,
Yet never fully satisfied.

Carrie Lindsay (13)
Antrim Grammar School

Openings

Can't think of an opening line,
It's hard enough to make it rhyme,
To write a poem you open your mind,
Open your heart, what do you find?

I haven't got anything, where shall I look?
I'm sure it would help to open a book.
So many openings, so many choices,
All muddled up like hundreds of voices.

If only I could open this door,
I'd be able to see so much more.
If I can't think of another line,
I'll resort to opening a bottle of wine.

How can I get myself inspired?
By that time I'll be retired.
Maybe I could think on the open road,
Open my eyes and lighten the load.

You probably need an English degree,
Perhaps from the Open University.
I guess this poem just can't be mended,
Why don't I leave it open-ended.

Ben Tisdale (14)
Antrim Grammar School

David

I have a good, close friend
He's like jelly and I'm ice cream
His voice is a hummingbird
I love the taste of his minty breath
He is so gentle with his hands
I like it when he hugs me
His smell is a rose sprouted by the sun
His looks are lovely and handsome
He is so romantic
Like Romeo and Juliet.

Susie Elliott (12)
Antrim Grammar School

The End

The heavens open
Down come fireballs
As big as boulders
And as hot as lava.

The sea crashes into Big Ben
As it floods over the country
Quicker than the north winds.

The wind sweeps over the world
Picking up everything in its way
Crushing it
Under its mighty force.

Lightning flashes in the sky
The great city of New York
Is lit up
With the flames of death.

Alexander Arrell (11)
Antrim Grammar School

Autumn

The air is getting cold and crisp,
The leaves are turning brown,
Acorns falling to the ground
And much earlier the sun goes down.

I do not like this time of year,
I'd rather have the summer,
It does not fill my heart with cheer,
I wish it could be warmer.

Then comes the winter season, so,
Autumn now has gone,
Wintertime brings the cold, white snow,
Another year is done.

Sarah Jane Kennedy (14)
Antrim Grammar School

Autumn, What Does It Mean To Me?

Autumn comes after the summer sun
And before the harsh winter.
Cooler days and darker nights,
Autumn, what does it mean to me?

Crisp, crunchy leaves
Falling from the trees.
Changing colours and windy days,
Autumn, what does it mean to me?

Toffee apples, apple tarts,
Bonfires and funny costumes
And Guy Fawkes.
Autumn, what does it mean to me?

Animals prepare for the winter ahead
And an extra hour in bed.
Hats and gloves soon appear,
As the winter draws near.
Autumn, what does it mean to me?

Andrew Patterson (11)
Antrim Grammar School

The Country

Grass gently swaying in the breeze,
Water trickling in the stream,
The sun shining in my eyes,
While I look at the big, blue sky.

Cows eating bright green grass,
Birds singing on the wires,
Farmers busy in the field,
While they collect autumnal yield.

As my walk in the country ends,
I plan to return another day,
I'll bring some friends next time around
And let them share the sights and sounds.

Geoffrey Campbell (12)
Antrim Grammar School

September 11th

September 11th is a day I'll never forget
It is a time of year that we all regret.
My dad was there,
It was hard to bear.

He was fighting through fire and smoke,
To try and save lives, how did he cope?
Smoke and flames up in the sky,
Many people wondering why.

Hundreds of people trapped up there,
Their future in tatters, with nothing to spare.
The rest of the people, heads down low,
Praying to God to let them know.

'Why did this happen?' the people say,
Let it be a dream, this I pray.
September 11th is a day I'll never forget,
It is a time of year that we all regret.

Catherine Lucas (14)
Antrim Grammar School

Dinner Time

Ketchup squirts
Peas boil
Sausages sizzle
While the grease goes dribble

The lid falls off the ketchup
The peas overflow
The sausages go pop
And Mum shouts, 'Oh no!'

Now Mum starts to boil
Her head goes pop
She shouts at us all
And tells us to clean up the lot.

Gemma Currie (12)
Antrim Grammar School

The Brave Macbeth

The weird sisters had an evil plan,
To poison the mind of brave Macbeth.
For he had great ambition and a good heart,
Which led him to his downfall and terrible death.

The sisters told him of a great future,
Of a great title and the throne.
He believed all the words the witches said,
So he worked his knuckles to the bone.

He performed the terrible murders of
King Duncan, Banquo and Lady Macduff.
These people were once his loyal friends,
But these deeds alone were not enough.

His friends rebelled, he was all alone
And into battle he had to go.
He fought his enemy, the good Macduff,
And lost his life to his great foe.

Victoria Burke (14)
Antrim Grammar School

My Direction

Walking somewhere, you don't know where,
Following a path leading to nowhere.
Needing to discover who to become,
Wishing to walk, but needing to run.

Feeling uncertainty build up inside,
Knowing the way, though unsure to decide
Which path to turn, what direction to go?
Still, deep down, you truly know.

You see imperfections, disregarding what you achieve,
You see only impossible, forgetting to believe.
Follow your path, release your inhibitions,
Know what you want and follow your ambitions.

Claire McCartney (13)
Antrim Grammar School

Goodbye

I can still see your smiling face
Your big, blue, twinkling eyes,
When I think of how it used to be
It makes me ache inside.

No matter where I went
I knew that you'd be there,
Now knowing that you've gone away
Is more than I can bear.

During those last few days
That you fought for your life,
You were so loved
As a mum, a granny and a wife.

As you lay on your death bed
You were like a little bird, so small,
And all I wanted
Was just to hear you call.

I knew you were scared
And it broke my heart,
I wanted to take you in my arms
And never part.

If I could have swapped places
Without a doubt in my mind,
I'd have taken your pain
And made it mine.

Your hands got colder
And as your blood pressure fell,
I knew it wouldn't be long
Until my life became hell.

I held you so tight
And I began to shake,
Your breathing shallowed
And I felt my heart break.

This was it
I was losing the best friend I'd ever know,
As you gasped for air
My tears started to flow.

As you took your last breath
A tiny tear fell from your eye,
You knew it was finally over
You were saying goodbye.

Jamie-Lee Culbert (16)
Antrim Grammar School

I Dream

As I drift away
Into the Land of Nod,
Things come rushing by
Of what happened that day.

When I sleep at night
I like to dream,
Of candyfloss clouds
And a chocolate stream.

When I sleep at night
I like to dream,
Of jellybean houses
And a rainbow beam.

When I sleep at night
I like to dream,
Of marshmallow people
And strawberry cream.

I dream that you will dream these same things,
Just like I do.
So don't be afraid to dream.

Gayle Allen (14)
Antrim Grammar School

Harvest Time

Harvest time is here again,
Lots of fields of golden grain.
Side to side and not a care,
Blowing in the breezy air.

The combine comes to do its deed,
The farmer is hoping for lots of seed.
Birds overhead are flying around,
Looking for food on the ground.

All the ploughing is now complete,
The drills in the field look so neat.
Potatoes are dug and sorted out,
Then taken to be sold, no doubt.

Daylight is shorter and the weather is cool,
Sheep must be glad of their coats of wool.
And then, like every year before,
All is safely gathered in once more.

Heather Clark (14)
Antrim Grammar School

Rainforest

As the rain pours down upon the damp forest floor,
As hot, humid steam seeps through the trees,
Trapped under the mighty leaves of the canopy's plants,
The tiny seedling burst.
Hidden by foliage, exploding with life,
Vivid colours slipping through the opening bud,
The stem straightened,
It stood.
The petals unfold and burst into bloom,
Red, blue, green.

Ellie Cameron (12)
Antrim Grammar School

The Fussy Eater

He doesn't think he is fussy,
Or that he is hard to feed,
Of fancy foods and sauces,
Just doesn't see the need.

His mum and dad are driven mad,
By his picky little ways,
He tells them he found something he likes,
It doesn't last two days.

They would like spaghetti Bolognese,
But he doesn't like the sauce,
They would eat almost anything,
Plain spaghetti is his course.

Chinese meals are what they love
And all sound kind of nice,
He would eat boiled chicken,
Served with plain boiled rice.

When they are eating their dinner,
It doesn't take them long,
They say he picks at his food,
When he's done, the night's half gone.

Even puddings are a struggle,
His list is not too long,
Put ice cream and jelly in one dish,
Then you have got it wrong.

Chris Molyneaux (13)
Antrim Grammar School

Christmas Time

A time of festiveness,
A time of goodwill,
A time of celebration,
Or a time just to chill.

The cake has been iced,
The turkey has been stuffed,
The tree has been trimmed,
But is that enough?

What's it about?
Is it just for fun?
We should appreciate Christmas,
Not just the pudding baked by Mum.

We should be thankful,
We should be pleased,
That years ago,
Our Lord, Jesus Christ, was conceived.

Laura White (13)
Antrim Grammar School

Bang!

Shotguns firing all around,
Sneaking about, not to be found.
Hiding in the bushes until I see,
The other side, a victim for me.
If he's in range, I point my gun
And believe me, this isn't fun.
I close my eyes and pull the trigger,
In front of the others, I'll look much bigger.
Bang! He's dead, straight through the heart,
How I really hate this part.
I run forward for a better view,
Bang! I'm hit - this part is new.

Jane Playfair (14)
Antrim Grammar School

Bugsy

I have a rabbit called Bugsy,
She is fat, but still very fluffy.
She is grey and white,
Has a big appetite
And is so cute and cuddly.

She sleeps all day
And at night she goes to play
With all her rabbit friends,
But sometimes it depends,
Whether a fox would come to stay.

I think Bugsy's great,
She is my best mate.
We play together,
No matter what the weather
And we love each other so much.

Rachel Walker (12)
Antrim Grammar School

The World Of The Paranormal

Do you believe in aliens
From planets far away?
Do fairies dance in your garden
At the very end of the day?
Have you ever seen a ghost
In the middle of the night?
Or looked up into the sky
And seen a strange and mysterious light?
What about the Pleiadians
Who live away far?
But how could anything
Live upon a star?
And then there's the monster of Loch Ness
The existence of these wonderful creatures
Is just a guess.

Rachel Steele (13)
Antrim Grammar School

The Sea

The sea sleeps calmly in a deep sleep,
As the wind passes by, it doesn't make a peep.
But soon the sleep will end,
As the wind comes back around the bend.

The sea sighs and rolls its eyes,
As the wind comes with a sudden surprise.
It shakes as it laughs when it sees the wind,
But soon will be heard far away in the sky.

The sea's eyes cross with anger,
For the sea has been awakened now.
The wind is still here, causing distress,
But it'll be a while till it gets a rest.

The sea puts up a brilliant fight,
But cannot fight all through the night.
The wind is scared away in fright,
So the sea laughs and says, 'Goodnight.'

Claire Williamson (13)
Cambridge House Grammar School

Tigers And Lions

Tigers roaring in the east,
Waiting to commence their feast,
Deer galloping to and from,
Roaming tigers, they will come.

Lions travel all around,
Looking to see what will be found,
Zebra, deer and antelope too
And all the things you find in zoos.

Back home they will rest,
With their manes like woolly vests,
In the morning they will wake,
Hunters near, so much at stake.

Shelley Malcolmson (12)
Cambridge House Grammar School

Butterflies

I love butterflies, I don't know why,
I think it might be because they flutter by.
They are beautiful and so pretty,
I wish they would play with my grey and white kitty.

They are the same on both sides,
But they have no eyes.
They are all different colours,
Bright ones and dark ones,
I love butterflies and I guess that's why.

Natasha McClintock (12)
Cambridge House Grammar School

Trouble!

Make the cauldron bubble,
Add the tails of two cats that cause trouble.
Throw in three wings of a bat,
Pop in a head of a rat.
Now the cauldron has begun to froth,
Mix some toe nails in this broth.
Stir and stir,
Add in some rabbits' fur,
Pour into a glass,
Don't forget to drink it fast.

Rachel McBrinn (13)
Cambridge House Grammar School

Old Man

There was an old man from Dundee,
He had a problem with wee,
It was very contagious,
He thought that was outrageous
And now he can hardly pee.

Luke Murphy (12)
Cambridge House Grammar School

A Spell To Make You Run And Hide!

A beetle's eye squeezed to juice,
Feather of vulture burnt to crisp,
Stir and stir, boil and bubble,
Lion's mane and baby boil,
Together this will make you cry,
Great white's jaw crunch and grind,
Eye of owl will make you howl,
Boil, bake, crunch, grind, squeeze,
Together this will make you run and hide.

Aaron Bailie (12)
Cambridge House Grammar School

The Sea

The sea is calm and silent in a deep, dark slumber,
The wind is the enemy that disturbs the water.
No more peace for now is war.
It pounds the rocks with its waves - the fists of steel,
It rolls into the shore
And sinks into the sand, never to be disturbed again.

Lois Neely (13)
Cambridge House Grammar School

Bill

There once was a man called Bill,
Who started to feel very ill,
Cos he thought he would risk it
And ate too many biscuits
And now he needs to get a pill.

David McMaster (13)
Cambridge House Grammar School

I Wish

If I could wish for anything,
I don't know what it would be,
Maybe to be the best hockey player,
Or maybe to be rolling in money.
But now it's time to stop thinking about me
And to think about other people,
So I wish there would be no killing
And no one be sad or unhappy.
But most of all I wish
That wishes would come true.

Kirstie Bruce (11)
Cambridge House Grammar School

My Limerick

There was an old man from Rudee,
He really loved to pee.
He pushed and shoved
And ate a slug,
He really liked chicken for his tea.

William Knox (13)
Cambridge House Grammar School

Mr Rea

A young man called Mr Rea,
Went for a walk one fine day,
It started to snow,
He exclaimed, 'Oh no!
Terrible weather for May!'

Adrian Hamilton (12)
Cambridge House Grammar School

Hurricane Phil

Quickly it hurtled through the street,
Howling as hard as it could howl.
Its arms spread as wide as they could
And picking everything up in its hands.

Angry eyes on the path ahead,
Smiling at the disaster.
It looks as if it is running,
It laughs as it passes by.
The end of the storm is here,
Hurricane Phil is dead.

Philip Simpson (13)
Cambridge House Grammar School

Thunder

Thunder booms like monstrous drums
Sounding deeper and deeper in the sky,
Darkness covers the world and light has said goodbye
Rain lashes and the wind howls, the earth is torn apart.
Destruction and mayhem, thinks the thunder, *it's a work of art.*
The chaos passes by and the thunder rolls away
The sun is now shining and the children come out to play.

James McConnell (14)
Cambridge House Grammar School

The Wind

The wind howls like a football fan,
It walks like an old man.
It blows the washing dry,
It waves at the children as it passes by.
It roars wildly like lions in a den
It whistles away into the sky
And that is the end of the wind.

Nicola Lorrimer (13)
Cambridge House Grammar School

The Train Station

The noise of wind on the leaves,
Plastic bags on the breeze,
Someone coughs,
Papers drop,
All is very calm.

Choo-choo, choo-choo,
Kids moan,
Mothers groan,
A person talking on the phone,
Doors slam,
People crammed,
All is not so calm.

Choo-chuga, choo-chuga, choo-chuga, choo-chuga,
Nana complains
About the train,
And what she'll say
To Auntie Elaine,
It's getting very busy.

Choo-chuga-whew-whew, choo-chuga-whew-whew,
The train comes,
People run,
Luggage tears,
Up the stairs,
'Quick, on the train!'
'Don't complain,'
'Find a seat,'
'Oh, my back's in pain,'
And *finally* we're on the train.

Rosalind Rowe (13)
Cambridge House Grammar School

A Handful Of Petals

A handful of petals
And sugar so sweet,
A drop of honey
Nice to eat.
A sprinkle of glitter
And diamonds so rare,
A bunch of flowers
To show that you care.
Put in the cauldron for twenty minutes
This potion will take you to the limit.
Take a sip, or two, or three
And this potion will fill you with glee!

Carole Duncan (12)
Cambridge House Grammar School

A Witch's Cauldron

Get the eyes of the cutest kitten,
In the cauldron throw a mitten,
Get the head of a cat
And the wings of a bat,
Collect the legs of a dog
And get the stomach of a frog,
Get a slimy snake and put it in,
Finish up with an evil grin! Moa ha ha ha!

Philip Gordon (12)
Cambridge House Grammar School

A Tiger That Came From Japan

A tiger that came from Japan,
Had the brain of a human man.
It ate Timmy Blair,
It choked on his hair
And put the remains in a can.

Jordan Cumberland (12)
Cambridge House Grammar School

Clouds

Clouds are fluffy,
Clouds are white,
Clouds are puffy,
Angels' delight.
Clouds are like cotton wool,
Soft and cuddly,
Angels rule.
Clouds are like big balloons,
But when they're dull,
Angels sad,
As crying rain starts to come.

Jason Gault (12)
Cambridge House Grammar School

Smarties

Blue, green, yellow, red,
All these colours in my head!
They look so bright, they smell so sweet,
Smarties are all I want to eat!
The shell is crunchy, the chocolate is munchy,
All you hear is crunching while you're munching!
Blue, green, yellow, red,
All these colours in my head!

Karen Munn (12)
Cambridge House Grammar School

Heidi, Justin And Dean Making It Clean

There once was a girl called Heidi,
She decided to make Ballymena tidy.
So she got her friends Justin and Dean
And said, 'Let's make this place clean.'
They worked till the end of the day,
The public said, 'Kids did this? No way!'

Steve Caldwell (12)
Cambridge House Grammar School

Just Thinking

I'm sitting in my bedroom writing this
Staring blankly at the TV as I try to concentrate,
Oh . . . wait, I just got a text from my mate,
He asked if I have finished my poem.

My favourite song is being played right now,
I'm not concentrating; just doodling and wasting my ink,
The dog barks outside; with all these distractions it's really hard
to think.
I wonder, will I get this finished in time?

I've just had a break from trying to write,
I'm trying to write again, but I'm just staring at the empty notepad.
I'd better get this written in time, or else my teacher will go mad.
I'm thinking of a few lines, but they're all really bad.

That's it, I'm turning off my TV,
No wait, this song is the best.
I give up, I can't be bothered
And I close the notepad and drop it against my chest.
Tomorrow, yes tomorrow I'll try again.

Daniel Cummings (14)
Cambridge House Grammar School

Limerick

There was an old lady from Leeds,
She always wore bright coloured beads.
She went out in the snow
And her beads they did glow,
What a wonderful sight indeed.

That little old lady from Leeds,
Had a little old cousin from Tweeds.
She worked in the town
And her husband a clown
And always for people did deeds.

Laura Rankin (12)
Cambridge House Grammar School

Lonely Night

Your hand slides out of its place with mine,
As the tears in my eyes shine, you have left me here alone
on this lonely night.
I am motionless, you are never coming back and I feel so empty,
I might just crack on this lonely night.
You turn back for that final glance, maybe this could be my
last chance,
But I doubt it on this stormy night, such a lonely night.
I am bewildered by my surroundings and the place around me
is at a standstill,
I can't bear this loss of you never returning.
Why is there so much pain in our world tonight?
Such a lonely night.
The fighting, the crying, the lying, the hurt.
The pain we are put through each day of our lives.
Love brought so many together and love tore so many people apart
On these lonely days, this lonely night.

Katie Crooks (14)
Cambridge House Grammar School

Life

Alone she walked down a dark street,
Searching for a path,
Although she thought there was no hope,
She kept on walking.

Further down the street a light shone,
She walked towards it
And found that she had hope,
She kept on walking.

Now she has a purpose in life,
She chose the right path,
She seems happy inside, but on the outside?
But she keeps on walking, just to see.

Amy Patterson (12)
Cambridge House Grammar School

Take My Life

He lingers in the shadows,
Fighting for his life,
Afraid of what's beyond the dark,
He is my mystery man.

People fear his staring eyes,
So deep and dark are they,
Feeding is his only joy,
My one mystery man.

His skin so pale,
His hair so long,
Nothing ever changes,
He waits alone for his victim,
My helpless mystery man.

He pounces,
He bites,
Deep into the throat,
As blood runs down the helpless neck,
He has taken my life.

Life and death are not his joys,
Seductive though is he,
He'll keep on living as they die,
My one mystery man.

Victoria Lowry (12)
Cambridge House Grammar School

There Once Was A Giant Hound

There once was a giant hound,
Who ran and jumped around.
He flew in the air
And he saw a pear,
So then he fell to the ground!

Leeann Gaston (12)
Cambridge House Grammar School

Tears

Tears come from sadness,
Tears come from joy,
Tears come from being kicked,
By naughty little boys.

Tears of pain come from
All those who are sick and lame,
Tears of joy come from happiness,
Wealth and fame.

Tears come near the end
Of a sibling's life,
Tears come from little cuts,
With sharp, dagger-like knives.

Tears come to my eye
As I finish writing,
Tears come from us all,
As the world is fighting.

Sarah Johnston (12)
Cambridge House Grammar School

I Wish . . .

Dear Fairy Godmother,

I've got a lot of things I want today,
I'll run and leap and play,
I'll have lots of fun today!
I wish for a jacuzzi full of girls,
With a beautiful beach full of pearls,
I wish for a bear who can cause a scare,
I wish for a boat, hydro powered,
I wish for a cat who can fly like a bat,
I wish for a bat who wears a hat,
I wish for a bed, I've got a sore head!

Rikki Gordon (12)
Cambridge House Grammar School

My Favourite Things

I have many favourite things,
But they're not all just money and rings.
My family for example,
I know it's just something simple,
But they're up high on my list
And every one of them would be missed.

Music also plays a big part
And I love it when songs go straight to your heart,
Or ones that cheer you up when you're feeling down
And just wipe away a frown.

Outdoors is somewhere I love to be,
There's so much to do and so much to see!
Staying inside just doesn't seem right,
Riding a bike or simply flying a kite.

Eating is something that can't be forgot,
But cabbage, broccoli and sprouts - definitely not!
Chocolate, strawberries and ice cream,
A chocolate-smothered heaven is only my dream.

My friends also make me laugh and smile,
At school or just to talk for a while.
At break, in class and at dinner time,
My favourite things all in a rhyme!

Joanne Fleck (14)
Cambridge House Grammar School

Sir Elton John

This person reminds me of a colourful patchwork quilt
And this person's colour would be a velvety purple.
This person reminds me of a chameleon.
If this person were a drink, they would be pink champagne.
This person isn't really who they say they are.
This person has often been compared to a wise owl.

Lesley Wilson (15)
Cambridge House Grammar School

Summer Is Over And Gone

All day long the hedgehogs are sleeping
And the rabbits have stopped leaping,
Christmas cards are in the shops,
It's too cold for ice lollipops,
Summer is over and gone.

No more water fights in the sun,
Back to school, away from Mum,
Santa's coming soon,
Flying over the silver moon,
Summer's over and gone.

Leaves are falling to the ground,
All sorts of colours - red, yellow, green and brown,
No more swimming in the sea,
Time for a nice warm mug of tea,
Summer is over and gone.

The sky is grey
And the swallows are flying away,
They'll come back some day,
Which will probably be May,
Goodbye summer, goodbye.

Melissa Campbell (11)
Cambridge House Grammar School

Winter

When I think of winter, it brings me many memories.
I am here to share a few with you.
The soft snow on the ground,
The quiet and peaceful sound.
Everyone playing their favourite jingle,
What will be the Christmas number one single?
A snowman standing all alone,
All these things tell me that spring has long since gone.

Jessica Boal (12)
Cambridge House Grammar School

Fingers

A wise pointer
A nose picker
An abusive sign
A ring holder
A breakable digit
A fork holder
A mouse clicker
A thumb war winner
A mistake pointer
A word follower
A button pusher
A trigger puller
A coin flipper
A vital part of everyday life.

David Cameron (15)
Cambridge House Grammar School

I Wish . . .

I wish I had a dog,
All of my very own,
I know it sounds quite selfish,
But is nice when you're alone.

I wish I had a pool,
To swim in all day long,
I'd have lots of my friends round,
Until the bell goes bong.

I wish a child could drive,
Along the city streets,
And when they have an accident,
The money grows on trees!

James Moore (11)
Cambridge House Grammar School

Wishes

If you had one wish,
Would you have some fish?
Or rather a cat
In a hat?
Money or the very best honey?

Would you think of yourself
And have the very best health?
Have a very big house
With not a single woodlouse?
Would you have a pool
With water that is cool?

Don't be selfish,
Share the wishes!
Have no more starvation?
Or more patience?
What do you want?
You decide!

Joanna Reid (12)
Cambridge House Grammar School

My Country

Lovely Lough Neagh
Go to the Giant's Causeway

Irish dancing
Lambs prancing

Fairhill shopping
Bunnies hopping

Pots of gold
It's often cold

Motorbike races
Friendly faces

It's Northern Ireland.

Emma Rose (12)
Cambridge House Grammar School

Noises

Noise, noise
Is a wonderful thing,
You can hear the wind blow
You can hear the birds sing.

A couple of things
I like to hear,
Is a cat purring
And a crowd's cheer.

But no matter what
I like to hear,
I'm happy that
I have my ears

To listen out
And listen well,
And a lot of the sounds
Can be swell.

Chloe Dalzell (11)
Cambridge House Grammar School

Feet

A mile walker
A comfort seeker
A smelly smell
A sweat breeder
A hard, crusty sole
A sock wanter
A shoe fitter
A world traveller
A personal transporter
A baby chew toy
Your personal friend.

Jonathan Small (14)
Cambridge House Grammar School

Hallowe'en

A flickering candle
A grinning pumpkin
A sudden fright
A midnight strike
A creaky stair
A vampire's lair
A grave digger
A dusty organ
A banshee's wail
An eerie song
A witch's broom
A haunted room
A crack of thunder
A firework explosion
A swooping owl
A distant howl
A dripping tap
A leaky pipe
A dark red stain
A decaying smell
A church bell
A spider's web
A laugh of something dead.

Rachel Allen (14)
Cambridge House Grammar School

I Wish

I wish to go to the world's biggest fair,
I wish to meet Man U's top player,
I wish that I had lots of money,
I wish that I was really funny,
I wish that I could fly
And soar up through the sky,
But the best thing that I could wish for
Is peace on Earth and no more war.

Michael Armstrong (11)
Cambridge House Grammar School

Terrorism

Terrorism is happening every year,
It fills nations with strife and fear.
The nature of the acts show that it is no error
And hence the name - all it does is inflict utter terror.

Terrorists shoot, maim and bomb and many people die,
Horrific explosions can be seen, causing structures to fry.
Why do they do it? What is the need?
Is it possibly for some selfish, unknown greed?

Terrorists must be full of evil, as their acts are inhumane,
They often hold innocents hostage,
Driving families frantic and insane.
Do they enjoy the destruction?
Do they like to burn things down?
Do they take pleasure in hearing screams throughout a town?

I really don't know what it's for, but I do know there is a cost,
In a single country, city or town, lots of life and love is lost.
I hope that someday this chaos will somehow peacefully stop,
Wouldn't the world be a better place
And the stench of corruption would certainly drop.

Glenn McGivern (14)
Cambridge House Grammar School

Hallowe'en

Bonfires, rockets, bangers and fright,
All dressed up as black as the night.
Ghosts, ghouls and witches abound,
The sky lit up with rockets and sound.
Bobbing for apples and ducking for treats,
Loads of children at play on the streets.
The bonfire's burned down, the lanterns are out,
Everyone's gone home without a shout.

Happy Hallowe'en!

Zachariah Deane (11)
Cambridge House Grammar School

Little Brothers

Little brothers, aren't they such a pain?
Little brothers, they are all the same.
Little brothers, some drive you mad,
Little brothers, they're not all that bad.

Little brothers, they can be quite cute,
Little brothers, you wish that they were mute.
Little brothers, they drive you up the wall,
Little brothers, you're glad you're not at the mall.

Little brothers, they look with prying eyes,
Little brothers, those eyes can make you cry.
Little brothers, but when they get mad,
Little brothers, they go straight to dad.

Little brothers, just when you think they're nice,
Little brothers, they hit you right in the face.
Little brothers, I'm running low on words,
Little brothers, now tell me all about yours.

Ben Houston (13)
Cambridge House Grammar School

A Magical Mystery Maze

Let me take you through a magical mystery maze,
Where the unicorns happily graze.
Come, come, we are going this way,
Look at the rainbow petals sway.
Watch this magical flier,
Can you see him go higher and higher?
Wait child, wait, please don't go,
At least let me give you a forget-me-not,
So you will not forget me!

Lauren Hannan (11)
Cambridge House Grammar School

Tornado

He's heading straight for me
I don't like his stare.
He's skipping over fences
As if he just doesn't care.

He's twirling around me
I'm caught in a trance.
If I stand here much longer
I'll not have a chance.

His eye dances round me
So silently still.
I'm caught in the moment
With this wonderful thrill.

Once again he's twirling round me
Caught again in a trance.
If I stand here much longer
I'll not have a chance.

The time has passed
And he's gone away.
Due to his madness
My people will pay.

Nikki Tweed (14)
Cambridge House Grammar School

Ode To A Pair Of Socks

Oh, wondrous socks, how I adore you,
How I adore your cosy cotton,
Your pink and white stripes make me treasure you.
You are my most precious choice,
I cherish you on the cold, cold nights.
You are a prized possession,
Not too big, not too tight,
Just perfect for my angelic feet.
You are a pair of socks,
My most cherished socks.

Samantha Campbell (15)
Cambridge House Grammar School

The Fairy

Watch as she flies high in the sky
Gliding and whirling as she comes down.
She whirls and twirls
And wears a beautiful gown.

She sparkles and shimmers,
Glitters and glows
And has a shiny golden crown.

She's got a tall wand
That glows and glimmers,
To wave around.
She swiftly moves but makes no sound.

Who could it be?
But the fairy.

Amy Lester (13)
Cambridge House Grammar School

Amy Lee

A shabby, shady seat,
A black satin sheet,
A ragged rug,
A Gothic guitar,
If she were a colour, it would be black,
Routine and schedule does she lack,
Mystery surrounds her being,
People are taken aback by her singing,
A princess of darkness,
An immortal spirit,
A ship going under,
She has everybody fooled,
An article waiting to be brought to life,
A fallen angel.

Ruth Barr (15)
Cambridge House Grammar School

My Mum

My mum has a small tum
And a lovely round bum.
She has good taste,
Which would be awful to waste.
With such good-looking eyes
And never tells lies,
That's my mum alright.

She is a brilliant cook
And loves to read a book.
She hates all bugs,
But gives lots of hugs.
She is really cool,
But hates the pool,
That's my mum alright.

She often does feel
That she can drive an automobile.
She really can't write,
Or fly a kite.
She hates all bees,
But she loves me,
That's my mum alright.

Denise McConkey (12)
Cambridge House Grammar School

I Wish

Fairy godmother, I hear I have five wishes
So this is what they will be!

I wish for world hunger to end, for I hate people starving
I wish for a fancy car and a big house too
I wish for no murder or suffering at all
I wish for a kinder world to keep this planet longer
I wish most of all to never lose my wishes
Or even lose you.

Michael Marshall (12)
Cambridge House Grammar School

Colours

The colours of the rainbow
The colour of my bed
The colour of rain trickling down
A dangerous colour like red.

The colour of the black sky
And the colour of my hair
The colour of pearly white teeth
The colour of a bear.

The colour of the yellow sun
The colour of the sea
The colour of a sunset
The colour of my tea.

The colour of my teacher's anger
And the colour of me
The colour of my best friend's smile
And the biggest heart that can be.

The colour of my blood
The colour of my face
The colour of my heart
The colour of my lace!

Feiona Stewart (12)
Cambridge House Grammar School

The Witch

I saw the witch of the west,
She really needed a rest.
I took her job,
Then my heart had a throb.
I wasn't a girl,
My hair didn't curl.
My nose was quite small,
I wasn't that tall.
So I bought her a vest
And now I'm the wizard of the west.

Jason Millar (11)
Cambridge House Grammar School

I Wish

I wish, I wish
I wish there was world peace,
There would be no need for police,
I wish there was no death when you grow old
And I could have lots of gold,
I wish I played for Man United,
I would be delighted,
I wish the world was good,
Just the way that it should,
I wish there was no evil,
Then there would be no upheaval.
I wish, I wish.

Neil Kennedy (12)
Cambridge House Grammar School

I Wish

Dear Fairy Godmother,

I wish I were a great director,
I wish there was no war,
I wish there was no pork and no homework.
I wish there was no money and bad people had no say.
I wish I had another wish so I would catch a fish.

Andrew Henderson (11)
Cambridge House Grammar School

Blue

I like blue,
It reminds me of Rangers
And salt and vinegar crisps,
The sound of the ocean waves
And the roaring at the Rangers' match.
But sometimes blue makes me feel cold
And I think that I'm by the sea.

Lauren Maxwell (11)
Cambridge House Grammar School

Horse

Some horses are tall,
Some are small.
Some like to graze
And some like to gaze.
Thoroughbreds are on the race track,
While trainers stand in the back.
Cobs pull carts
While Arabs are in the ring.
Andalucians get all the attention,
But Oldenburgs are best at extensions.
We can't begin to imagine the trust they have in us.
Horses have been the most important thing in a man's life.
We owe them a great deal of gratitude.

Stephanie Simpson (13)
Cambridge House Grammar School

Darkness

In the night there is no light,
There is nothing in your sight,
Nothing that is bright.
The colour is pure, dark black,
Like a big sack of coal,
The sound outside is like a ghoul.
The whistle of the wind,
Only a few lights -
The moon, stars and street lamps.
I like looking at the dark sky,
I wish I could fly.
At night I like getting tucked up in bed
And that is what I said.

Jake Eaglen (11)
Cambridge House Grammar School

Autumn

Summer is gone,
Autumn is here,
The ghosts and ghouls
Will soon appear.
The leaves are falling,
Orange, brown and gold,
The nights are darker
And it's getting cold.

I love the fireworks,
Going bang in the night,
They light up the sky
And might give you a fright.
We knock on the doors
And play trick or treat,
They give us some money,
Or maybe a sweet.

I always love this
Time of year,
When the ghosts and ghouls
All appear.

Robert Waddell (11)
Cambridge House Grammar School

Harvest

The crops are cut
The trees bear nuts
The golden leaves fall down
As gardeners frown
The darker nights
The Hallowe'en frights
The fireworks explode in the sky
The women making apple pie
The rain falling down like lots of tears
The animals hibernating till summer is near
Harvest is an exciting time of year.

Nicole Erwin (11)
Cambridge House Grammar School

I Wish

If I had a fairy godmother,
I would ask her for the following things:
I wish for a safer world so we can all live in harmony and peace,
Or what about no more animal and child abuse?
I wish for poor people to have food,
Now that would be really good.
I wish for no more deaths,
Because they just make your life a mess.
I wish for no more crying,
Or what about no more lying?
I would like all these thing to happen,
But I know in this life not all of this is possible.

Laura Frew (11)
Cambridge House Grammar School

Dusty

I have a dog whose name is Dusty,
He has big, dark brown eyes,
He is quite dopey and is a very disobedient dog,
Who likes digging holes in the garden.
He drinks loads of water
And likes eating his dinner,
He's not domesticated,
He's like the Devil in spirit.
He's not very dependable,
He always demands attention,
He may be a dopey, disobedient brat of a dog,
But I love him.

Simon Morton (13)
Cambridge House Grammar School

Noise

I like noise
I like the sound of a choir
Laaa

I like the sound of sheep
Baaa

I like the sound of the teacher saying no homework
No homework

I like the sound of a parrot
Squawk

I like the sound of the orchestra triangle
Ting, ting

But most of all I like the 3.20 bell
Brring, brring.

Megan Wilson (11)
Cambridge House Grammar School

The Lovely Little Lethargic Lam

The lovely, little, lethargic lamb,
Leaps lively around the large field.
It limbers through the long, lush grass,
Lazily it lies down along a hedgerow
And it falls into a deep sleep.

Slowly the little lamb awakens to a lifeless world,
All the creatures of the world are dead.
A luminous nuclear bomb fell and left the area leveled
And the lovely, little, lethargic lamb is now all alone.

Adam Robinson (13)
Cambridge House Grammar School

The Car

Slowly the car drove out the driveway, only to break down.
It really was a heap of junk, the owner knew it all.
It didn't really want to go, it hardly started at all.
But when the owner said, 'You'll go to the scrap heap for sure,'
The car jumped into action.
It almost drove into the wall.
Its arms were opened wide,
Until it stalled once more.

Samuel Bradley (13)
Cambridge House Grammar School

My Dog

Tara is my dog,
She likes to chew a log
And annoys a cat called Mog.

She likes to pull clothes off the washing line,
It can be fine,
But sometimes they are mine.

Tara is very smart,
She runs like a flying dart
And she has a very big heart.

Nicola Watson (12)
Carrickfergus College

Nicola

N ice and smart
I ntelligent, sweet and kind
C ool and does not fuss over anything
O utrageous and sometimes crazy
L aughing and always smiling
A nd she will always be my friend.

Paige McAuley (11)
Carrickfergus College

What Is That Smell?

Oh, what is that smell?
I'd love to know, I'd love to smell it
Wherever I go.

It's not the smell of dirty sludge,
It's more the smell of home-baked fudge.

It's not the smell of bacon sizzling,
It's more the smell of dewdrops glistening.

It's the kind of smell that lasts in your nose,
Just like jumping into bed with just-washed clothes.

It's definitely not the smell of Belfast Zoo,
It's more the smell of a barbecue.

No, it's not the smell of Phoenix Gas,
It's more the smell of freshly cut grass.
It's not the smell of beef jerky,
It's more the smell of Christmas turkey.

I know it's not the smell of days old coffee,
It's more the smell of sticky banoffee.

It's the kind of smell that lingers long,
It makes me want to burst into song.

Do you know the smell of a dirty PE kit?
Well, I'm almost sure it couldn't be it.

How can you find out what this smell is about?

When I'm seventeen the time will be near,
Let's hope that it will not be too dear.

I hear you ask what on earth this could be,
Just be patient and you will see.
So sit back, relax and enjoy the ride,
If you're lucky, I will let you inside.

It's the smell I'll own if I work hard,
It's the smell inside a *brand new . . . car.*

Andrew Patterson (12)
Carrickfergus College

Winter

It was a blistering cold winter's night
The creaks on the dusty floorboards
Gave me a fright.
The glowing moon was nowhere in sight
And the growling wolves were having rough fights.
The discoloured leaves were blowing
On the willow trees
And the beautiful geese were flying wild and free
On the soft breeze.
And now the shimmering snow is coming down swiftly
It's a practical winter's night and snowmen are out.
Christmas trees are gleaming bright
And the stars are shining out tonight
So goodnight, goodnight.

Sophie Rush (11)
Carrickfergus College

Emma Rosbotham

Emma is my name
Marvellous and energetic I am
Making things and reading are what I love to do
And my best friend is Nadine Todd.

Roses and white lilies are my favourite flowers
Organised and ready for anything
Strong and beautiful I am
Brilliant at maths and English
Others I always put first (most days)
Happy and cheerful all day long
Africa is where I would love to go
My way, it's my life.

Emma Rosbotham (11)
Carrickfergus College

It's Raining

It's raining
It's raining
I'd like to go out and play

It looks so exciting
I would play all day

The rain is pouring and soaring out of the sky
People are running as fast as they can
Trying to get out of the rain

I hear children playing, talking,
Shouting and screaming

It's raining
It's raining
I'd like to go out and play.

Chelsea Meeke (11)
Carrickfergus College

Rathlin

I climbed up the hill
And saw a wee goat,
Then I went to the harbour
And saw a big boat.

We went into the sea
With my canoe,
The sun was so bright
And the sea was so blue.

All over the island
I would happily roam,
And on the last day
I went on the boat home.

Sam McIlroy (12)
Carrickfergus College

The Fabulous White Hart Lane

The fabulous White Hart Lane
So big and crowded

Brilliant enjoyment and outstanding
Like a massive, gigantic mansion

It is like a large pyramid
I feel like it is life

I feel like it is the best of the lot
And that everybody notices it

The fabulous White Hart Lane
Reminds us of a winning team.

Brent Stockman (12)
Carrickfergus College

An Ode To Old Trafford

I loved Old Trafford, it was cool,
Even better, we weren't in school.
The football ground was massive,
My friends will tell you that,
It was massive and that's a fact.
Everyone loved it,
We all had a blast,
But we weren't on the grounds
'Cause it was out of bounds.
I told my dad that it was mad,
I bet he was jealous,
But he won't tell us.

Lucy Cooke (12)
Carrickfergus College

Myself

My name is Aaron Carley,
I really hate fruit and barley.
I have two sisters and no others,
And I don't have any brothers.

I live in Coronation Crescent,
But it isn't much of a present.
My school is Carrick College,
You have to have good knowledge.
My favourite film is '8 Mile',
Because Eminem has a good style.

My favourite football team is Liverpool,
I think they are really cool.
They're nothing like Man U or Arsenal,
They're just full of big, ugly men in all.
Rio Ferdinand got banned from playing,
He was lazy and didn't go to training.
He's back playing early,
So he should think himself lucky,
I heard he still has a little yellow ducky.

Aaron Carley (11)
Carrickfergus College

My Poem

Football is the greatest
If you're good it will bring you fame.

Liverpool are my favourite team
To play for them would be my dream.

Michael Owen is no more
But how I love to watch Gerrard score.

Watch out Arsenal, you're going down
We're going to blast right through your town.

All other teams are filled with fear
Because we're going to win the league this year.

Daryl Ingram (12)
Carrickfergus College

Trick Or Treat

'Trick or treat, trick or treat,
Give us something good to eat.'
This is what the kids all shout,
The night the ghosts and ghouls come out.

Screech, bang, crackle,
The fireworks have exploded in the air
And all the kids stop to stare.

Kids dunking for apples
And eating monkey nuts,
This is what we like to eat,
On the night of trick or treat.

Tracy Foster (11)
Carrickfergus College

Autumn

The leaves are falling off the trees,
Brown, orange, yellow,
Blown down by the wind,
Lying on the ground,
All around.

I love to run through the leaves,
Crunching under my feet,
Kicking them about,
Lying on the ground,
All around.

Glen Robinson (11)
Carrickfergus College

Winter Haiku

Bright stars shine like sparks,
Eyes glitter in shop windows,
The town's like winter.

Jordan Ferguson (11)
Carrickfergus College

Nadine Todd

N adine is my name
A nd Emma is my best friend.
D uring school hours,
I like to make people laugh,
N ever lie to the teacher,
E nergetic and love playing.

T alkative and I have a sense of humour,
O h, how I love sunny days,
D on't talk back,
D aisies are my favourite flowers.

Nadine Todd (12)
Carrickfergus College

Mustang

M onster of a car,
U nlikely to go off road,
S trong car to race,
T raditional in the inside,
A ttractive looking car,
N aughty looks,
G rowls from the engine.

Leigh Johnston (11)
Carrickfergus College

Autumn

A utumn leaves fall off trees
U ntil winter comes
T rees grow bare
U nder the trees lie all the coloured leaves
M any children gather conkers
N ow it's time for hats, scarves and gloves.

Alice Cole
Carrickfergus College

Liverpool

L iver bird on our chest
I nto Europe we will go
V ictories we shall seek
E uropean cups we have won
R eds roar on every week
P eople watch around the world
O wen is gone but not forgotten
O n and on we shall go
L iverpool will always be in my heart!

Stephen Grant (11)
Carrickfergus College

Summer

S ummer is a time of laughter and fun
U nder a clear sky with plenty of sun
M emories of holidays far away, long hours on the plane,
   also life on the farm
M ore fun when we get there in tractors and sleeping rough
E ating barbecue chicken and hot dogs
R eminding myself of summer times makes me joyful and happy.

Mark Deering (12)
Carrickfergus College

My Chelsea Poem

C heering them on
H ome or away
E xcellent team
L egendary players
S tamford Bridge their home ground
E ndless triumph
A lways scoring goals!

Scott McKinty (11)
Carrickfergus College

Springtime

S pringing little lambs
P rancing around the dams
R inging their little bells
I n and around the wells
N o one to stand and stare
G oing here, there and everywhere
T ime is ticking by
I nfants crying
M other feeding
E at away and then off with the little lambs.

Colin McKinty (12)
Carrickfergus College

Chelsea FC

C helsea is the team I support,
H ooray, we're in the Champions League,
E idur Gudjohnson is a brilliant striker,
L ampard is my favourite player,
S tamford Bridge is their amazing stadium,
E very year they get beaten by Arsenal,
A bramovich is their billionaire chairman.

Nathan Poulter (11)
Carrickfergus College

Spring

S pring is the time when birds sing
P arks are full of children playing
R ivers flow in spring
I n the fields the lambs play
N ature is now at its best today
G rowing buds are starting to flower.

Amy Reid (12)
Carrickfergus College

Great Minds

G reat minds working away to learn
R eading all day and night
E very second of the day
A lways working away
T oo much to learn

M ore time needed
I nformation taken in
N o time to play
D igging deeper every day
S o much to learn.

Steven McAlister (11)
Carrickfergus College

The Raining Poem

R uining the day
A lways raining, never stops
I n and out of puddles, young children jump
N owhere to hide from the everlasting rain
I n the house being shouted at by their mum
N ever stops. Bored in the house.
G ood for a water fight.

Josh Barron (11)
Carrickfergus College

Sport

S cotty Parker is the man 'cause he runs as fast as he can.
P atrick Viera keeps to the plan and he tries as hard as he can.
O n the pitch the players are good because they eat the right food.
R onaldinho has the tricks, nobody thinks he is thick.
T revor Sinclair skins them all, that is when he is on the ball.

Matthew McFaul (11)
Carrickfergus College

School

Waiting in my form class
For registration to begin.
Teacher telling pupils
'Put your gum in the bin.'

Waiting for the bell to ring
To get to my first class,
Want to get there quickly
So I'm not the very last.

Hunting through my school bag
For my ruler, books and pen,
Writing the date on pages
Time and time again.

At last the school bell rings
Out the gates we run,
To cars and trains and buses
There's homework to be done.

Rebecca Poh (12)
Carrickfergus College

Time

Time goes on and on,
Time is short and time is long.
Time to go and time to come,
Time to be silent and time to talk,
Time to run and time to walk.
Time for sport and time for work,
Time for pleasure,
Time for leisure.
Time for new and time for old,
Time for happy, time for sad,
Time for good and time for bad.

Time for my rhyme
To end!

Jason Allen
Carrickfergus College

Salima

I know a girl called Salima,
She's as sweet as a girl can be,
But sometimes she can be cheeky
And rages in anxiety.

Her mood is like the seasons,
It's odd, but true.
But when she finds a true friend,
She'll stick to her like glue!

She's really good at heart,
And she'll give you a great start,
On how to spend the day
And just go ahead and play!

So mind what I say,
She's a pretty girl all day.

And you'll surely never miss,
After you read this,
That Salima is the best
And above all the rest.

Salima Azad (11)
Carrickfergus College

Puppy To Pooch

The day I got my puppy,
Was a very exciting day
And when we drove up to the house,
My heart just skipped a beat,
'Cause when I saw my puppy dog,
I fell in love with her.
And to this day I love her
More than I have ever done before.

Rebekah Mayes (11)
Carrickfergus College

Rain

The lights are on, it's just past midday,
There are no more indoor games we can play,
No one can think of anything to say,
It *rained* all yesterday
And it's *raining* today.
It's grey outside and inside me is grey,
I stare outside the window, fist under my chin,
When they say to cheer up, I imagine a grin.

Samantha Mogey (11)
Carrickfergus College

Mars Bars

M is for milky
A is for adorable
R is for really tasty
S is for scrummy

B is for *buy one now!*
A is for all kids like them
R is for reasonably priced.

Amy Harrisson (11)
Carrickfergus College

Sunflower

She stands so tall from a seed so small
Planted in hope that come summer
Her smiling face will appear
Turn to the sun
And then bow to the moon come dusk.

Stuart Winsby (12)
Carrickfergus College

In The Dark Trying To Sleep

It was dark
I could not see a thing
All I could hear was a dog bark
Trying to get asleep was very hard
I tried and tried for nearly an hour
Listening to the noises in my backyard
Then at last I got asleep, all was quiet
In the street
Not a sound, not a peep.

Rebecca Cambridge (11)
Carrickfergus College

The Moon

I love to watch the moon at night,
Because it shines so very bright.
I hate it when the clouds pass by,
Because it makes a dark, dark sky.
I often wonder what it's like,
To sit upon that moon at night.

Natasha Hill (11)
Carrickfergus College

My Mum

M y mum is great
Y es, she is even better! She is excellent

M y mum is a peace sign
U wish you had a mum like mine
M y mum is like a taxi driver and a chef.
    She would do it all day.

Gemma Spence
Carrickfergus College

School

School sometimes can rule,
Other times it's a fool.
If you do your work fine,
Then you won't get lines.

If you stay on the right side of the teachers,
Life will be great,
But if you don't,
You'll be staying in at break.

It can be fun as long as you say,
'Oh hey, Sir, hope you have a nice day!'
But if your manners don't stay all through the years,
You may end up in very bad tears.

So school can rule as long as you,
Keep up the behaviour and don't miss school.

Rebecca Rea (11)
Carrickfergus College

I've Lost You

I have loved and lost and cried and cried,
Because of the time we had kissed in the church
And hugged under the bridge,
I will miss you.
Now you are dead, but I will remember you
And love you always.

I'm happy again, I'm living my life,
I'm about to get a wife.
As I watch over your grave,
I will miss you forever,
I always have and always will
And I will meet you in Heaven
Where we can start over again.

Sam Mitchell (12)
Carrickfergus College

Hallowe'en

As I walk down the street,
Going door to door,
Trying to get a trick or treat,
I'm afraid to explore.

Masks, wigs and scary things,
Bats and witches
Are all part of Hallowe'en.

Fireworks go on through the night
Even when I'm tucked up tight,
Small animals become afraid
Even if their owner is very near.

I'm very keen on Hallowe'en,
It is my favourite time of year,
And now it is very near,
I'm wondering,
What will happen this year.

Michael Finlay (12)
Carrickfergus College

School Life

Tick-tock goes the clock on the classroom wall,
Ring, ring goes the bell in the staring hall.

Sing, sing go the kids racing out the door,
Joy, joy for the teacher locking the classroom door.

Sleep, sleep in the night, silent as can be,
Brring, bring goes the clock in the morning time,
It's time to go to school again,
It's time to rise and shine.

Sarah Chism (12)
Carrickfergus College

My First Day At School

I didn't know what to do
I was going to a school so new.
I lay awake at night in bed,
I couldn't get it out of my head.

I was up very early on my first day,
I was ready for what was to come my way.
I left early to catch my bus,
I left early so as not to be in a rush.

How long is this bus going to be?
There it is now, behind the tree.
I was happy that I was on my way,
This was a very exciting day.

I saw some people I already knew,
And some I didn't, there were quite a few.
I saw the school down the hill,
My tummy felt a little bit ill.

I got off the bus after a while,
And walked into school with a smile.
The school was so big that day,
Thankfully, teachers showed me the way.

My first day was really great,
My school bag was a ton weight.
I couldn't have chosen a school any better,
It just keeps getting better and better.

Jordan Robinson (12)
Carrickfergus College

Hallowe'en

Hallowe'en comes this time
Every year,
It gives you a fright and
Fills you
Full of fear,
Ghosts, ghouls, witches and
Black cats,
Pumpkins, vampires
And bats.

Fireworks banging into
The
Night,
Sparklers twinkling with
Lots of
Coloured light,
Children come to trick or
Treat
To try and get some sweets.

Candy apples, nuts and
Treacle toffee
Are the things
That makes me happy,
I love Hallowe'en with its
Spooky ghosts,
But dressing up is what I
Love
The most.

Danielle Burns (11)
Carrickfergus College

Ice Hockey

Tonight is the night
We go to the game,
To meet with the others
Who think the same.

To cheer the boys
Who play in white
And maybe we'll see
A good old fight.

The team in white
Is the Belfast Giants
To them ice hockey
Is a form of science.

The formula with which
They skate around,
Knocks the other team
Onto the ground.

As Curtis Bowen skates up the rink,
We all then start to think,
Will he score, he just might,
Or will he get himself into a fight?

He scores a goal,
We jump with glee,
We leave the game,
And go for tea.

Ethan Clarke (11)
Carrickfergus College

My Scrambler

My scrambler is speedy, like a cheetah chasing its prey.
My scrambler is loud, like a fog horn.
My scrambler is green, like a lizard.
My scrambler is dirty, like a wild pig in a bog.
My scrambler is my scrambler.

Christian Shanks (11)
Carrickfergus College

Dogs

Dogs are cute and cuddly
They can be any shape or size
Big and small
They can be in any colour
You can even have a pink dog
You can have a really fluffy one
Or a short haired one or a long haired one
You can have a dog with dreadlocks
You can have a really big dog or a really
Small dog.

You can have a dog with a short tail, long tail,
Curly tail
There are country dogs and town dogs
You can have a trained dog or normal dog
You can get a dog with two breeds.

Just like my dog Buff!

Sushanna Marshall (11)
Carrickfergus College

The Winter Sky

On a winter's day,
I love to go out and play,
Throwing snowballs on the way.
'You can't get me!' all my friends say.

So many footsteps in the snow,
And all the snowmen in a row.
I bent down low to make a snow angel,
But at home I'm no angel!

I saw the snowflakes falling from the sky,
They came from somewhere up so high.
Oh how I love the winter sky!

Elaine Boyd (11)
Carrickfergus College

Hallowe'en

Children happy, all dressed up,
Sky up above them all lit up.

Bonfires and fireworks light up the sky,
As rhyming children pass us by.

Cracks and bangs and whistles and 'Wows',
Noises around us that everyone knows.

Ducking for apples and the singing of songs,
Everyone's laughter drives the night on.

The sky becomes silent; the streets are all cleared,
The noises and laughter have all disappeared.

The Hallowe'en party has come to an end,
The witches and goblins have all gone to bed.

But if you look up to the dark sky at night,
You still might see something that gives you a fright!

Michael O'Hare (11)
Carrickfergus College

A Poem On My Sister

J is for Julieanne my sister
U is for unicorn because they are beautiful like her
L is for love, it is the thing that she does best
I is for intelligent that is what she is
E is for egg, a thing that she likes to eat
A is for amazing that's what she is to me
N is for negative, but she never is
N is for never, she never lies
E is for exams, she always does well.

Stephanie Mooney (12)
Carrickfergus College

Making Music

Piano, flute, band and choir,
In my lifetime I desire,
Fun and laughter all my days,
Love and passion in different ways.

Piano you learn by notes and scales,
C to B and F to G.
Practice time means shorter nails,
Making sure you do not fail.

Flute is fun, you press the keys,
Out comes air, and don't you sneeze.
Make sure you press the proper keys,
So that you learn just how to please.

Band is cool, you play your part,
Making music that touches the heart.
Music stands with notes held high,
As our music reaches the sky.

In choir you get taught how to sing,
Hitting the notes is my thing.
First and second sopranos bring,
Melodies fit for a king.

Gillian Scott (11)
Carrickfergus College

Clothes

C lothes are used for wearing and to keep us warm
L oose trousers around our waists are better
O ther clothes are designer ones for movie stars
T housands of people wear clothes but some people are
   unfortunate and don't get them
H ow do the people that make them make so many different kinds
E veryone needs clothes
S o go out and spend, spend, spend!

Matthew Calwell (11)
Carrickfergus College

My Boring Cat

My cat is so boring!
He lies around from night to morning.
He sits on his comfy chair,
With no sound of a single purr.

He's black and white just like midnight,
With round eyes like clear blue skies.
He has socks white and snowy,
But walks and runs really slowly.

He sleeps from nine to five,
And sometimes I don't know if he is alive.
We took him round to the local vet,
And we have found the best cat we've ever met.

He has changed his mood,
And he eats all his food.
He's begun to eat
His fish and meat,
And that's better than before.

He's not so boring after all,
He plays around with his bouncy ball.
He seems to always get so cosy,
And now and then he still gets dozy!

Joelene Cooper (12)
Carrickfergus College

Seasons

S ome are sunny
E ven some are windy
A utumn has crispy leaves
S ummer is full of heat
O n top of a mountain
N ever look down
S easons are here every minute.

Thomas McCord (11)
Carrickfergus College

School

School . . . school,
Why is it so boring?
During all your classes,
You may as well be snoring!

The only part I like,
Is when we get let out,
So we can go outside,
To run and jump about.

Oh no! The bell has rung,
That is such a shame,
Maybe we could go out tomorrow,
And continue with our game.

Now we are out,
What a tiring day.
In fact I actually quite like school,
Too bad the classes get in the way!

Jordana Donnelly (11)
Carrickfergus College

Cute And Cuddly!

Dogs are lovely,
Cats are nice,
Dogs lick your hands,
And cats chase mice.
Goldfish swim around the bowl,
Rabbits hop and foxes howl.

Budgies cheep and hamsters run,
They give their owners so much fun.
I love my pets,
They are my friends,
They are so loyal,
Right to the end.

Victoria Deacon (11)
Carrickfergus College

Summer

I like to travel to far away places,
To see the sights and different faces.
Sometimes the plane journeys are so long,
But when you arrive you feel you belong.

I went to Florida, it was a blast,
Took ages to get there, but the time went fast.
Disney World was my favourite place,
Although I did go to NASA and saw space.

In the summer I went to Spain,
It was hot and sticky but it didn't rain.
We spent a lot of time in the pool,
It was much more fun than going to school!

Now I'm home I miss the heat,
All I have is the winter and sleet,
But next July, when the holidays start,
I'll be off to Spain, even if it's in a horse and cart.

Hannah Waite (12)
Carrickfergus College

Rain

Splishing, splashing raindrops,
On my windowpane.
Little robin redbreast,
Singing in the rain.

Two little children out to play,
With little red water-boots, hip hip hooray.
Splishing, splashing in the rain,
Up the street and back again.

Claire McLaughlin (11)
Carrickfergus College

My Doggies

Ben is like a big bear,
He is covered with lots of hair.
When people see him they always run,
When all Ben wants is to have some fun.

Lady is the fantastic one,
As all she does is play and run.
Lady loves to fetch a ball,
She comes a-running when I call.

Daisy next and that's them all,
She never likes to fetch a ball.
'Daisy Woo' is her nickname,
She loves to mess and play a game.

So those are my dogs,
They jump about like frogs.
They are all my loveable dogs.

Rachel McKnight (11)
Carrickfergus College

My Dog Joey!

He chews his bone,
Runs around
And cries when he is all alone.

His mouth is big,
His tail is long,
And he dances when he hears a song.

When you tickle him on the chest,
He feels as if he's just the best,
That's my dog Joey!

Megan Wilson (11)
Carrickfergus College

No Sound

One lovely
Cold winter
Night such
A fright. It
Was around
I was standing
On the ground
Looking around
There was no
Sound. It was
Like the place
Was out of
Bounds. Just until
I found a message
On the ground. That
Said we'd found what
We were looking for.
I had a frown. What
Happened without
A sound?

Demi Smith (11)
Carrickfergus College

The Sun

Over the grass that swishes and swashes,
Over the trees that sway in the breeze,
Over the rooftops, mine and yours,
Over the hills and the mountains,
At night I sleep,
In the morning I rise,
All day long I beam in
Surprise!

Lois Passmore (12)
Carrickfergus College

Dogs

They start off so small, but grow to be tiny or tall.
They're cuddly and hairy and some a bit scary.
They can be brown or black or white or spotty,
Shy, loud, or even a little dotty.
They're faithful and true and love only you,
With us to the end, a faithful, true friend.

Lana Turner (11)
Carrickfergus College

Love And Hate Diamante

Love
Beautiful, sweet
Loving, kissing, caring
Stunning, nice, hit, grump
Hitting, stealing, complaining
Horrible, bad
Hate.

Christina Burns (11)
Dunclug College

Land And Water Diamante

Land
Grass, houses
Running, talking, looking
TV, Playstation, float, relax
Sinking, swimming, running
Blue, cold
Water.

Terence Donegan (11)
Dunclug College

School And Home Diamante

School
Boring, rubbish,
Talking, writing, listening,
Homework, extra work, TV, PS2
Playing, eating, sleeping,
Peaceful, quiet,
Home.

Stuart McCarthy (11)
Dunclug College

Work And Play Diamante

Work,
Hard, difficult
Learning, reading, spellings
De-merits, detention, computer games
Running, singing, laughing
Fun, enjoyable
Play.

Catherine Chambers (11)
Dunclug College

Night And Day Diamante

Night
Dark, spooky,
Sleeping, turning, crying
Sleep, quiet, light, morning
Playing, eating, shopping,
Bright, relaxing
Day.

Krystina Boyle (11)
Dunclug College

Coldness And Heat Diamante

Coldness
Blue, freezing,
Freezing, chilling, shivering
Chill, frost, warm, hot
Roasting, boiling, sweating,
Red, warm,
Heat.

Jennah Bonnar (11)
Dunclug College

Fire And Water Diamante

Fire
Boiling, bright
Blinding, melting, eye-catching
Hunter, destroyer, friends, saviour
Soothing, sparkling, extinguishing,
Cold, smooth
Water.

Joseph Elliott (11)
Dunclug College

Club And Home Diamante

Club
Wonderful, fun
Doing, visiting, meeting
Play, have fun, TV, PlayStation
Playing, sitting, eating
Boring, sleeping
Home.

Steen Graham (12)
Dunclug College

These Shoes

These are the shoes
In which my mum
Dragged me kindly
To school!
I was wearing these shoes
When I played
With my friends
In the muck,
When I chased
My bestest ever friends
Outside on the rough tarmac
I wore these!
These are the shoes
That I fell when I was
Going very, very fast
Whilst playing with my friends.
I learnt to ride my bike
While I wore these shoes,
When I wanted to stop
I just trailed them
On the mucky ground.

Robin McNabney (14)
Dunclug College

Heat And Coldness Diamante

Heat
Warm, cosy,
Fiery, sleeping, tiring
Sunny day, sun foundering cold
Freezing, icing, snowing,
Sore, runny
Coldness.

Zoe Donnelly (11)
Dunclug College

The Shoes

These are the shoes
In which I used to sprint
Like a cheetah chasing its prey.
Whizzing swiftly around the
Track in the 200m final
After my friends who annoyed me.
These are the untied shoes
I fell in, when I walked,
Then my dad lifted me
Up as high as the clouds.
My fantastic Mum cuddled me
Like a teddy bear,
When my shoes were invisible to the eye.
I smacked the ball
As hard as I could
At my friend's nose.
Sprinting like a maniac
Around the living room.
These are my special shoes
That helped me walk like
A pony taking its first steps,
And I've cherished them ever since.

Christopher Blair (13)
Dunclug College

My Diamante Poem! Diamante

Love
Warm, married
Loving, kissing, hugging
Beautiful, lovely, ugly, horrible
Disliking, disgusting, annoying
Bad, furious
Hate.

Nadeem Khan (11)
Dunclug College

The Shoes

These are my favourite shoes
I used as a pair of brakes
When I was going fast on my bike.
These are the shoes
I wildly kicked my brothers with
When we got into a fight
Over a toy or a bag of sweets
Making us feel like three monkeys
Fighting over a banana.
When I bounced
On my granny's sofa.
These are the shoes with which
I could rise to the fluffy clouds.
When my tummy rumbled
Like a lion
That hadn't eaten in a week.
These are the shoes
That assisted me in reaching
The biscuit tin,
Making me feel that
I was wearing stilts.

Neil Backus (13)
Dunclug College

School And Home Diamante

School
Boring, dull
Answering, listening, writing
Homework, extra work, TV, PS2
Playing and texting, sleeping
Relaxing, warm
Home.

Ashleigh McDowell (11)
Dunclug College

The Shoes

These are the shoes
That kept my feet dry
During the winter months.
These are the shoes
That let me keep my grip like an army tank
On that ice covered path
Then I started to run on
And I ran too fast and slipped like a clumsy big ape
And fell
I cried for my dad
And my dad came in a matter of seconds.
He took me home
And gave me a wonderful big bowl of chicken soup.
These are the shoes
That he took off me
As he tucked me into bed
And then read me a bedtime story
And then said
'Goodnight' and then turned off the light
And kept the door open
Enough for a bit of light to creep through it.

James Shaw (13)
Dunclug College

Cold And Warm Diamante

Cold
Freezing, chilly
Slipping, snowballing, coughing
Sore, painful, fine, well
Roasting, boiling, scalding
Hot, sweaty
Warm.

Erin Spiers (11)
Dunclug College

The Shoes

These were the small green wellies,
I wore running madly,
Through those massive green fields
Belonging to my aunt.
The wellies were the ones
I wore walking casually
Around snowfilled forests and roads.

While wearing my green wellies
I put a snowman together.
I nastily chucked large
White snowballs towards my
Younger brothers and sisters.
Unsuccessfully they tried
To dodge them
As they ran through that deep snow,
As high as kites,
On that cold winter's night.

Debbie McDowell (13)
Dunclug College

Day And Night

Day
Bright, sunny
Playing, laughing, smiling
Fun, great, scary, horrible
Running, hiding, looking
Creepy, dark
Night.

Rebecca Nicholl (11)
Dunclug College

The Shoes

These are the shoes
I wore when we travelled to the zoo,
Dad cautiously gripped my hand tight
And swung me onto his shoulders
Where I could see everything
And grasp the fluffy white,
Cotton clouds.
These are the shoes
I danced around in
Happily pursuing ducks in the park.
With bread to feed them.
The tattered and ragged shoes
I wore when I went shopping with Mum,
How my tired feet throbbed
After those never-ending trips to the town.
These are the shoes
I have long since forgotten
And I'll leave them behind, go on my way
For another to find.

Thomas McGuigan (13)
Dunclug College

Sweets And Drinks Diamante

Sweets
Sugary, bitter
Chewing, swallowing, sucking
Sticky, toffee, watery, runny
Drinking, spilling, gurgling,
Clear, drinkable,
Drinks.

Lisa Blayney (11)
Dunclug College

My Shoes

These are the shoes
In which I learnt to walk
That I got
For my first birthday
The shoes I wore
When I got gently pushed
To my granny's house in my pram
To show her my new shoes.
These are the shoes
I tripped in
Chasing my sister
Round the park.
My granny quickly lifted me
And cuddled me in the dark sky.
These are the shoes
I got measured for
In the shoe shop.
These are the shoes
I wore when I fell
Down the slide
Like a bungee jumper
With no rope
And I'll remember them
Forever!

Ashley Kernohan (13)
Dunclug College

Cat And Dog Diamante

Dog
Quiet, tame
Jumping, playing, walking
Beautiful, good, horrible, bad
Spitting, chasing, killing
Noisy, vicious
Cat.

Melissa Millar (12)
Dunclug College

The Shoes

These are the shoes,
In which I happily circled the garden
When my mum played chasing.
These are the shoes
That crawled slowly into the kitchen
Of my nana's house,
And my dad ran after me
So I wouldn't hurt
My hand on the wooden door.
When I tightly held onto my dad's hand
When I quickly crossed the busy road,
I wore those shoes.
These are the shoes
That lifted up from the hard ground
As high, high, high as a hot air balloon,
As I tiptoed trying
To peer into the zoo cage.
These are the shoes
That made me come last,
Like a tortoise
In running races on sports day.
These are the shoes
That I chose when I got my feet measured
And I'll keep them forever.

Sarah Rusk (13)
Dunclug College

Sun And Moon Diamante

Sun
Hot, bright
Shining, heating, scorching
Fireball, star, planet, round
Beaming, glistening, gleaming
Cool, clear
Moon.

Rory Welsh (11)
Dunclug College

These Are The Shoes

These are the shoes
Which helped me cycle faster and faster
Like lightning
On my bike.
When I was whizzing around
The fairytale garden
Laying on an ancient bed sheet.
These are the shoes that
When we saw uninvited strangers
Let me hide
In my dad's wall-like legs.
These are the shoes
I wore when I saw my first thunderstorm
Harsh rain,
Flashing car headlights.
These are the shoes
On that frightful bridge
Like walking the plank
With me in them.

Kyle Nicholl (14)
Dunclug College

The Shoes

These are the shoes that ran in circles
That stood on my dad's legs
And kicked like a football player
To get out off the pram,
And scuffed when I fell.
These are the shoes
That trampled Mum's straight shoulders
Which swung below the kitchen table,
That climbed over furniture.
Which bounced around the house,
That dropped off when I went to bed.

These are the shoes.

Matthew McKeown (14)
Dunclug College

The Shoes

These are the shoes
That carried me like a rocket
Around my grandparents' sanctuary,
The shoes I tumbled
Down the steep steps in,
The shoes that swung loosely
On my feet
Like leaves on an autumn tree
When my popsie lifted me up to the sky.
When he gently cleaned my knee
With a hug and kiss,
But now I'm older,
And my feet are clown-sized
And those shoes
I've come to miss.

Joanne Surgeoner (13)
Dunclug College

The Shoes

These are the shoes
That Mum told me I was getting.
That I went to Antrim with Granny.
I went to the shoe shop
A girl came over who had a great big
Smile and measured my feet.
Then because of a space between
Two stools, in which I was sitting on
I fell over like a drunk man.
Kicked the girl up the teeth.
She said 'Ow!' I said 'Wha!'
Then I saw Granny picking me up.
Then the girl said 'I'm OK and
Your shoe size is small six.'
I just smiled. What else could I do?

Nigel McMullen (13)
Dunclug College

The Shoes

These are the shoes
I widely threw around.
These are the shoes
That made me fall to the ground.
These are the shoes,
You couldn't see
When I rolled through the mud,
Like a pig.
These are the shoes
That were all wet,
When I splashed through the pond
When I thought I was a duck.
These are the shoes
That made everyone think
When I threatened
To throw them
In the damp kitchen sink!

Lyndsay McPhee (13)
Dunclug College

The Shoes

These are the shoes
I dropped down the loo
Dad fished them out with a spindly stick.
My nail fell cleanly off in.
These are the shoes
That rapidly left the ground like rocket ships
Blasting off
As I touched the sky.
The dog
Tried to eat them
When we bought her home
From the kennels.
These are the shoes
That I have kept lovingly in my trunk.

Phillip Tynam (13)
Dunclug College

The Shoes

These are the shoes
That helped me,
Quietly tiptoe round,
When my sister was
Snoring her head off.
These are the shoes
That left the rocky hard ground,
When lifted up
Into the sky
Like a kite
Up high,
By my dad
After kicking the football
In the park.
These are the shoes
When whizzing loudly
Round and round
In a shop
I'd slide and fall
My knees all cut
And my mum putting
A plaster on it,
Like a nurse
With her patient.
These are the shoes
That when playing
Hide-and-seek
With my dad,
Would guide me
To catch him.

Kerry Quinn (14)
Dunclug College

Autumn Stir Fry

Preparation time   9 months
Cooking time   6 months
Serves   Entire population

Ingredients
One medium sycamore tree
Two splashes of icy frost
A handful of serrated auburn leaves
Two large glossy, juicy, gleaming
apples washed and cut.
A sprinkle of wind and rain.

Method
Stir fry glacial snow and brunette foliage
For a night,
Add a sprinkle of depression and a long night.
Leave to hibernate for three months.

Serve over a sweltering amber blaze with
Optimistic drink, piping hot.
Wrap in a warm rainbow of happiness
Blended with coarse shrubbery until
Smooth.

Now ready to serve.

Blaithin Buckley (12)
Our Lady Of Lourdes School

If The Rain And The Snow Had Feelings

Clouds are slothful in their movement as though
The nip in the air embodies every bead.
The chill seems to make time itself sluggish;
As the overhead lake of diamond soldiers;
Begin their treacherous quest to the earth.

Many die as their limbs explode against unyielding rock.
Their severed bodies blend into thousands more;
To form a pool of glazed blood. This is swallowed
By a glutinous sucking soil with no soul,
Never taking time to mourn the quenching source.

Others have crystal parachutes to gently
Float to safety. Most drown in the river of blood.
The few survivors then perish in the blistering
Glow of the blinding sphere from east of the sky,
Leaving nothing, except a sea of bodies.

In the end the life of a diamond soldier
Is fickle. Parachute or not, the results
All correspond to give the same conclusion.
Not all is lost. Some are chosen by the
Blinding sphere resurrected and travel again.

Christine McClements (14)
Our Lady Of Lourdes School

True Love

True love is a feeling,
I just can't ignore.
Cupid awaits to open the door.

With his arrow poised,
Aimed at my heart,
It was then I knew,
That this was the start.

From the beginning, so magical,
To where we are now,
Love, affection, honesty and trust,
My heart's definitely telling me this is a must.

We laugh, we cry,
Through good times and bad,
He makes me happy,
Even when I'm sad.

With love so strong, it's convincing now,
I've found my soulmate,
My one true friend
All I ask is that this never will end . . .

Jenny Bamford (15)
Our Lady Of Lourdes School

A Poem For Chocoholics!

Milk and plain even white
Are all the chocolates that I like
And as I need an everlasting supply,
To this little poem I apply,
Give me an endless flowing stock,
Of . . .
All my favourite bars of choc,
And whilst I'm committing this
Hungry sin,
Keep me gorgeous and incredibly
Thin!
I don't care about sugar levels
Or butter and fat
I really love chocolate
And that is that!

Bridget McGinty (14)
Our Lady Of Lourdes School

Mobile Phones

Mobile phones they are so great
Boys and girls can ring a mate,
Messages, games, calculator and clock
Everyone now can talk, talk, talk.

Mobile phones they are useful too
For friends and family to contact you,
Or if you're far away and lost
A ring on the phone is little cost.

Mobile phones they are quite small
They fit in your pocket with no trouble at all,
The only thing you need to fear
Is how quickly your money can disappear.

Samuel Clark (12)
Parkhall College

Alone!

Sitting here all alone,
The thoughts go through my head.
Thinking of all the good times,
And the bad times you have had.

Being alone is painful,
And really scary too,
You don't know what it's really like
Until it happens to you.

I think it hits you worse at night
It makes you want to cry,
And sometimes it gets really bad,
And you wish that you could die.

So listen to what I gotta say
And don't crawl under a stone,
Because believe me friends, I know just what it's like,
When I talk about being alone.

Jodie Taylor (12)
Parkhall College

In The Dark, Dark Town!

There was a dark, dark town
And in the dark, dark town there
Was a dark, dark street
And on the dark, dark street there
Was a dark, dark house
And in the dark, dark house there
Was a dark, dark room
And in the dark, dark room there
Was a dark, dark cupboard
And in the dark, dark cupboard there
Was a dark, dark box
And in the dark, dark box there
Was a dark, dark ghost!

Laura Foster (13)
Parkhall College

Knitting

Knitting is my hobby
I can knit scarves long and short,
And blankets wide and round
It's fun because it's interesting and skilful.

I've knitted one scarf before
It keeps me really warm
When I'm outside in the cold
Or in the pouring rain.

I can knit all day while watching TV
It's not that hard just practise and you'll be good.

When I'm bored at home
I just take my knitting out and just
Knit, knit, knit.

Symone Cullen (12)
Parkhall College

My Footy Poem

This poem is about my football team
Who I think are so class
They score less goals that other teams
But still I think they are class.

They have some brilliant players
Who score some smashing goals
Thrash some teams who are easy
And lose to those so hard.

Sure they're nothing special
They haven't won the league
They're not the best team in the world,
But still I think they're class.

Chris Adamson (12)
Parkhall College

Three Months

January is like winter but
Warmer and better.
The leaves are like crisps,
All crunchy and brown.

March is a happy season
Like people going out and
Having fun.
Little lambs being born.
Their mums and dads getting
Their coat shaved off.
Their coat is as white as snow.

December is slippery
So be careful
It is like you are on an ice rink.

Nadine Brownlee (12)
Parkhall College

My Dog Sindy

My dog Sindy is one year old
When I got her she was small and bold
A treasure never to be sold
I'd never leave her in the cold.

My dog Sindy is the best
Better than all the rest
When she sees the cat go by
She's sure to give it a lovely goodbye.

My dog Sindy hates having baths
So when I am finished she has a mud bath
I do not get angry, I just laugh at her
As she is my pet and I love her.

Robert Clyde (13)
Parkhall College

9/11

It happened on that fatal day
The two Twin Towers were blown away
People were buried beneath the rubble
Boy that day caused loads of trouble.

People ran people screamed
This was worse than I could have dreamed
People watched with disbelief
While others wailed and cried with grief.

As the planes hit the buildings they burst into flames
I don't understand the terrorists' aims
One man called Bin Laden brainwashed these men
Who knows when he'll strike again?

Hundreds of people on those planes
Plenty to lose but nothing to gain
Little did they know that day?
Their lives would be so tragically taken away.

Thousands lost their lives that day
All in the name of God they say
To me it seems very odd
How can this be done in the name of God?

Rodger McLaughlin (12)
Parkhall College

Mums

Mums are so bossy
They don't let you have fun
Mums are so strict
They ground you
Mums are so annoying
They make you eat vegetables
Mums fall for your dad
They start to ignore you
The best thing about mums are
That they love you.

Ashleigh Thorne (13)
Parkhall College

Normandy

As I lay down on the beach
Hearing the bombs and guns go off
The Germans fight for power
As we fight for freedom.

Bodies lie asleep
All over the beach
Red sand everywhere
Some caused by me.

Running up the hill
Trying to conquer land
Shooting Germans
Hoping for the best.

One year later
Hitler is dead
The world is at peace
Hope it stays that way.

Matthew McKenna (12)
Parkhall College

My Poem

This poem is for my coursework
I have to do it well
For my teacher, publisher and me as well.

This poem is for my test
I will try my best
And hopefully I will do well.

People thought I was stupid
But I will prove them wrong
With this poem it will be in this poetry book
For so long.

Gary Hume (13)
Parkhall College

Our Wee House

Our wee house is a great wee house
It's built with bricks and stone
The only thing that's wrong with it
Is our wee dog Tone.

He chews all the locks
He eats all our socks
He never can seem to keep still
But we know he could if he will.

We always try to train him
But he never seems to listen
We're always so close to take him back
But we know that we'll miss him.

Our wee house is a great wee house
It's built with bricks and stone
The only thing wrong with it
Is our wee dog Tone.

Jodie-Lee Gould (13)
Parkhall College

Silent Night

As I lie in my bed at night
I always wonder what is happening outside.
As the trees sway and branches crack,
I always wonder what happens at night.

As it's dark and dogs bark,
Babies cry as creatures fly.
People commit crime,
As quick as time.

As I lie in my bed
In the silent night
If I was younger
It would give me a fright.

Simon Mellon (12)
Parkhall College

Seasons

Spring
The sheep are as happy as a mother
With a newborn baby when her lambs are born.
The lovely daffodils were as bright as a light bulb.
The snowdrops were as white as a ghost.
The leaves were as colourful as a rainbow
In the sky.

Summer
The sea was as calm as a baby sleeping.
The sun shone like a burning fire.
Playing about and having water fights is like a shower
In April.

Autumn
The time for falling leaves,
They flutter in the breeze,
Autumn makes me sneeze.

Winter
Snow is lying on the ground,
See my footprints all around.
My hands are cold,
My nose is red,
I can't wait till I'm tucked up in bed.

Chantelle Waite (13)
Parkhall College

A Dog's Life

Whatever it was I didn't do it
I was in my bed
If they ever find me
I may as well be dead.

It started early this day
I was in the kitchen
Having my morning snack
When my owner's son came in
Oh what an ugly sack
When at once he tripped and fell
And hit the kitchen shelf.

A problem began all at once
I thought I had better hide myself
When my owner came he asked
'Who in blazes did it?'
His son at once said 'the dog'
And at that second trouble began
The anger in him had lit.

So this is why I've hidden right now
In fear and in anger
For now you know the reason why
I am definitely for it.

Adam Boyd (12)
Parkhall College

The House!

I'm all alone in a house
The wind is howling loud.
I hear some scary noises
And footsteps that are loud.

I look out the window
I see shadows passing by
I wonder what they really are
Is there danger nigh?

I run downstairs
And into a room
I hear more scary noises
I hope they will stop soon.

In the garden
I can hear
People screaming
Sounds like fear.

In the bedroom
Lights flicker off
The scary noises
Again start off.

Victoria Walker (12)
Parkhall College

Silly Sam's Slippery Snake

Silly Sam bought a slippery snake
But silly Sam's snake was so slippery
It slipped out of silly Sam's hands
So silly Sam's snake was on the floor
So silly Sam chased after his snake
But silly Sam slipped and went
Sliding across the floor
Silly Sam caught his slippery snake
Now silly Sam doesn't old his
Slippery snake anymore.

Kayleigh Melville (12)
Parkhall College

Football Poem

Football is my favourite sport
It's a great game to play
I play it with my mates
I seem to play it every day.

I really like Man U
I don't know about you
I really enjoy football
What about you?

I like to watch the matches
It's great to see them win
I sometimes tease my mates
But sometimes it's a real sin.

I guess you heard it all
It's time to say goodbye
I hope you liked this poem
It was written by a Year 9.

Aaron Mitchell (13)
Parkhall College

Christmas!

I love the sound of Christmas
That winter always brings,
Everyone has great fun,
So everybody sings.

Snowdrops in the garden,
Everyone's in the house,
Outside where snowmen are
It's as quiet as a mouse.

When you go back out,
Have fun whatever you do,
Whoever you are with
Make sure they all have
Fun too!

Shauna Jones (12)
Parkhall College

Seasons

The first season of the year - winter.
Cold and chilly like standing in a big fridge freezer.
No matter how many clothes you put on
You're still dripping with icicles.
Spring is bright and exciting like newborn lambs.
Now the weather has changed slightly.
It's brighter, more colourful like a rainbow in the sky.
Summer has arrived once again.
It's like standing in a sauna when you go outside.
You can have barbecues late at night,
And you can sleep in because there's no school to go to.
But my favourite season is autumn.
When leaves fall from the trees like rain falling from the clouds.
Sparrows and house martins suddenly disappear.
But others return like the robin.
But it's winter again the worst season
At least Christmas is just round the corner.

Victoria Clements (13)
Parkhall College

Sadness

Sadness makes you feel empty inside.
Sadness is like the last time I cried.
When you're sad, you feel confused
It's like being hurt and abused.
Sadness is a feeling
It's one that hurts.
It's like being bullied and pushed in the dirt.
Sadness can't just be pushed aside.
It's like when someone cries.
Sadness is like a hole in the sky.
Sadness is something that makes us sigh.

Leanne Adams (13)
Parkhall College

Sadness And Fear

Sadness hurts, fear stings
Unhappiness is what it brings.
Sadness is a bat, when it hits you it may hurt
Like being thrown in dirt.
Fear is a black shadow in the middle of the night
Your hairs on your arms stand on their ends
When you get a fright.
Sadness causes a lump in your throat, fear is contagious
People think it's outrageous.
Do you know what it feels like? Have you been there?
Sadness is a bear, it's everywhere.
Fear is a prickly hedgehog
It makes you jumpy like a frog.

Christina Maher (13)
Parkhall College

Sadness

Sadness is like someone dying
Sadness is like someone crying
Sadness is like a bird being shot
Sadness is like being dumped on the spot
Sadness is like being hurt and abused
Sadness is like being shocked by a fuse
Sadness is like being bullied at school
Sadness is like being beat at pool
Sadness is like being lost and found
Sadness is like losing a pound
Sadness is like people who lie
Sadness is like the last goodbye.

Lauren Scott (13)
Parkhall College

Happiness

She's as happy as a boy at a football match
As happy as an American at the World Series,
She's as happy as a dad to see his son's first goal,
When she's on her horse.

She's as happy as a dog to see a new owner,
As happy as a father to give his daughter away to marriage.
She's as happy as a mum to see her child go to college,
When she's on her horse.

She's as happy as a teacher to give an A,
As happy as a pupil to get one,
She's as happy as a cat with a fresh bowl of milk,
When she's on her horse.

Aaron McLean (13)
Parkhall College

My Football Fantasy

I want to be like Milan Boras,
I want to be able to play for my favourite club
In the whole wide world, Liverpool.
Boras is a goal machine!
He is like a younger version of Pele the wonderkid.
I even dream of scoring goals like him.
He is the best; he was the top scorer in Euro 2004.
I will be like him one day just wait and see.
I will be in the Liverpool team
That would just complete my dream.
It would feel like I'm dancing on the clouds
Singing in Heaven
I will be the new Liverpool number seven.

Stuart Mitchell (13)
Parkhall College

The Seasons

The flowers are blooming like rockets.
The leaves are back on the trees,
All the baby animals are born, especially little sheep,
If you remember the horse chestnuts are growing,
And you wait for them to sprout,
Now you know what time of year it is? It's springtime.

The weather outside is grand, the suntan lotion is out.
When the sunrays are hitting your face and you're wearing
a sweatband.
All the children are off school to play and do as they please,
You know what time of year it is? It's summer.

When the leaves are falling like cats and dogs,
And the flowers are starting to die,
When all the woodland animals start to make their beds
For their sleep that last months,
The little hedgehogs are sleeping, so are the badgers and bears,
So you know why it's so quiet now?
Autumn is here.

The weather outside is frightful.
Inside the fire is so delightful.
When the blustery winds are blowing
And the snow is glowing and glowing,
Like the skies are falling from Heaven.
You need to be careful, because winter is here.

Chris Mowbray (12)
Parkhall College

My Old Oak Tree

My old oak tree just as sure,
Has leaves and flowers that are ever so pure,
Its branches are like witches' hair,
All swirly and squiggly.
The tree's roots are skeletons' fingers,
Crawling up through the ground.
There's a hole in the middle, like a face just watching you,
Everything you even do.
On the branch there is a swing, it looks like an earring.
There's wrinkly marks on the trunk which is more of
A wrinkly person.
The tree's trunk is like a giant drinking a can.
Inside I built a room, the same as the one I have at home.
At Christmas I decorate it to make it look better,
It is as beautiful as the town Christmas tree.
The tree's leaves are like cactus pricks.
The fruit that grows on it is as juicy as the ones
At the supermarket.
Everything is just perfect about my old oak tree!

Amy Gibson (13)
Parkhall College

Fear

Fear is ghosts in the night
Out to scare little kids.
Fear is vampires out to suck blood off people's necks.
Fear is ghouls flying about your house
Screaming their heads off.
Fear is zombies in the night
Out to kill.
Fear is spiders crawling up walls
And all over you with eight great, big, hairy legs.
All of these fears we learn to overcome.

David Pritchard (12)
Parkhall College

Seasons

December the month for Christmas,
This is an alphabet about Christmas.

C is the candy trimmed around the Christmas tree
H is the happiness for all the family
R is the reindeer prancing by the windowpane
I is the icing on the cake as sweet as sugar cane
S is for stockings 'neath the tree so tall
T is the toys for all the boys and girls
M is the mistletoe where everyone is kissed
A is the angels who make out their Christmas list
S is the Santa who makes every kid his pet.

Be good and he'll bring you everything
In your Christmas
Alphabet.

Louise Rooney (13)
Parkhall College

My Puppy

My puppy is a boxer, with fur as soft as silk
Her name is Leah.
Everyday I let her out to play,
She hops and skips like a kangaroo, because she is so happy.
She has a basket full of toys, just like a baby.
She picks a toy and I wrestle with her,
She is as strong as an ox,
When she hears the gates open she knows my dad is home
From work.
I really think she loves my dad the best
Because she licks his face as if it was an ice cream
But I still love my puppy the most
'Cause when she is happy, I feel happy.

Naomi Whann (12)
Parkhall College

Fear

Fear is as frightening as a haunted house
Fear is when you're scared of a mouse
Fear is when you see a ghost
Fear is when you're frightened the most
Fear is when you shake like a leaf
And when you're confronted by a thief.

And then the clock ticks twelve,
And a book falls off the shelf.
The branches bang against the windowpane
As if there's someone there in the rain.
You pull the covers over your head,
As if there's something under the bed.
Is there anyone there?
Then you wake up and it was just a nightmare.

Rachel Stewart (13)
Parkhall College

Sport

He is as happy as a boy at a football match
He is as happy as a boy playing catch.
A football is so round
When you score with it you should hear the sound.
The giraffe is as high as a basketball net
Who will score first? The fans have placed a bet.
The rugby ball is shaped like an oval
The pitch is as long as a snake.
The baseballer hit the shot far.
He must hit it with some power.
The hockey ball is as small as a mouse.
The hockey net is as tall as a house.
In indoor football kick it high, it's over head height
Do that in outdoor, it's out of sight.

Adam Jackson (13)
Parkhall College

Sadness

The weather is bad,
It's very, very rainy.
I thought this was madness
And so did Jeff Blainey.
Our class was going wild.
The clouds were big buckets of water
Just ready to pour down on us.
I go to the window with my best friend Gus,
The weather was wild,
But it's changing to mild.
My heart was filled with sadness
But slowly it's filling with gladness.

Matthew McCauley (13)
Parkhall College

My Auntie Janet

She is as thin as a rack,
As fast as a car,
As strong as an ox,
As proud as a peacock,
As obstinate as a mule,
As hungry as a wolf.

Hair like hay,
Hands like claws,
Ears like cauliflower,
Legs like matchsticks,
A neck like a spoon,
A head like a balloon.

Stephen Elkin (13)
Parkhall College

You're My Angel

You're the angel
From my dreams,
I speak the truth
To me you gleam.

All around you,
Is a golden light,
That lifts my heart
So that I take flight.

Your eyes are deep
They're of the sea
Your hair is golden
The fairest, it be.

Tall and handsome
Brave and strong,
Please hear my words
Please hear my song.

You're just a dream
This I know,
But where you dwell,
Always I'll go.

Heather Cosby (12)
Parkhall College

Happiness Is Like A . . .

Happiness is like a butterfly,
Flying in the sun,
Like a bird that's free
To fly to the horizon.
It is like a dog,
Running crazy
Or like a bee
Buzzing around.
Happiness is like a lamb
In its field
Happiness to me is the
Best in the world.

Laura Mairs (13)
Parkhall College

My Cat Smudge

I have a cat
Her name is Smudge
She's such a playful pet
She rolls, she jumps
She races about
And often attacks my toes
You would think she was totally mad.

And yet at night
She's a different cat
All sleepy, content and relaxed
Curled up on my bed
With her head on my knee
That's how I like to go to sleep
Just her and me.

Sarah Curry (13)
The Wallace High School

Messaging

(Dedicated to Jake Stanley, Stephen Clarke and Jodie Brown, without whom this draft would not have been achieved)

(One message received)

A day apart, but I miss you already.
Sparkling eyes, warm smile,
Gentle arms holding me tight.
Happiness, security, comfort, love . . . completeness.

Stars above us, earth below us,
Everything before us - together forever.
Long weeks apart but a whole lifetime as one.
The heart grows fonder.
I can wait.

Day is near. I count the seconds
'Til you're beside me - sweet breath
On my neck, gentle lips on forehead,
Fingers running through hair,
Embracing my loved one.

At the station now; an hour to go.
Platform crowded, seats broken - doesn't matter.
All I want is to have you here,
To see your face,
Be reunited at last.

Still waiting - no train has come.
Delay? My heart pounds.
Something wrong? Mouth runs dry.
Hurt? No; unthinkable.
Answer, my love. Answer me.

Final message, but no reader now.
No reply this time, or ever again.
Screen is blank, life is empty; all is lost.
Nothing left to wait for.

(Inbox empty)

Caroline Hynds (16)
The Wallace High School

Isolated

This is just a skeleton diagram of my lonesome land,
Where darkness roars and I've been stranded.
The soft pad's down and the hard front's up,
It stands strong against the corrupt
But has been broken down and infected these cuts.

Distance will arise out of your selfless lies
Lost in these dreams.
Out of your world, awake yourself in surprise
Of a tasteless dryness as crying prides of my land digress.
I'm suppressed.

No more new us living in broken trust,
I say no more when you say I must.
I'm at breaking point, weak and dizzy,
I can't let go of my clinging history's shame.
You seal yours in silence and forget my name.

Turn and walk away from us,
Flood this land with fairytales in miraculous voices
That adjust and manipulate my choices.
Well my land has no choice and causes no fuss.
It will crumble.

Nicky Parks (17)
The Wallace High School

Spiders

Huge, hairy,
Creeping, ugly,
It's scuttling quietly around
My bedroom floor,
Darting to and fro.
I'm petrified as it comes towards me . . .
Trying to escape my bedroom.
Screaming, running away
Shaking . . .

Lyndsay Creswell (12)
The Wallace High School

Who Likes School?

Who likes school?
All you have is annoying teachers,
the feeling that everywhere you walk,
people are going to push or shove you
because you're younger than them,
conducts,
rules,
being made to sit beside annoying boys,
tests,
exams
revising,
maths . . .
geography . . .
embarrassment in many ways
I don't think so!

But hold on . . .
I suppose you do get to hang around
and talk to your friends,
have the friendly atmosphere,
having ages for break and lunch,
discos,
doing art and music,
having *some* nice teachers,
free periods,
making buns,
merits,
actually being allowed to eat crisps instead of just biscuits,
not having your legs go dead because you sit too long,
getting out of the house and away from your parents' guard,
maybe I do!

Emma Davidson (12)
The Wallace High School

Creeping Through The Amazon Jungle

Creeping through the Amazon jungle,
Dodging trees and slithering snakes,
In the Amazon, snakes and creepy-crawlies lurk about so,
Watch out!
Giant spiders, tiny bugs, huge snakes, tiny snakes, scuttling
All about.

Creeping through the Amazon jungle,
Listening to the squawking birds,
In the Amazon jungle parrots of many colours up in the trees
Big birds, small birds, beautifully coloured, dull coloured,
Flying all about.

Creeping through the Amazon jungle,
Hearing the cry of a baby monkey wanting to be fed.
In the Amazon jungle the monkeys are in hundreds up in the trees
Enormous apes, tiny monkeys, black ones, grey ones, brown ones,
Orange ones, up in the trees.

Creeping through the Amazon jungle,
Petrified at the rustle of anteaters all around.
In the Amazon jungle are vacuums of anteaters at breakfast,
Lunch and dinner,
Long snouts, short snouts, fat ones, thin ones, down on the ground.

Creeping through the Amazon jungle,
To hear the thud of trees as they hit the ground,
In the Amazon jungle the chainsaws of lumberjacks cutting down
The trees,
Loud chainsaws, quiet ones, fat lumberjacks, thin ones,
Destroying the Amazon jungle!

Andrew Cummings (12)
The Wallace High School

Wasps!

Yellow and black,
Hairy and mean,
Constantly buzzing
Ever so keen.
Mean looking eyes
Small as can be,
As they hover over the flowers
Quite contentedly.

Innocent child eating ice cream
The wasp moves in,
Quietly it moves through the air
Lands on his arm,
Move, will he dare?

He froze to the spot
Not risking to move.
He bites his lip and begins to run,
Sting, he cries out for his mum!
For no reason a wasp can cause pain,
Then fly off and do it again.

Callum Curry (13)
The Wallace High School

Injections

Injections
Long and thin
Terrifying, agonising pain,
As it approaches my heart races,
My palms are beginning to sweat,
I feel like I'm going to faint.
The needle is so long and sharp
Yet again so terrifying,
I am told not to scream but I can't help it.
Those stupid needles.
Injections.

Caroline Davis (12)
The Wallace High School

My Dreaded Doom!

Her piercing green gaze,
Her crooked warty nose,
My English teacher
Her mind-numbing voice as it echoes through the room,
My English teacher
Her mind racing thoughts,
Her spiteful words,
My English teacher
Her spine-chilling presence,
Her lean, claw-like fingers,
My English teacher
Her hair-raising shrill when she laughs
Her bone-crunching cruelty
My English teacher
Her stomach-churning smell,
I cannot wait for this lesson to end because of . . .
My English teacher.

Caroline Ferguson (12)
The Wallace High School

Pizza

My favourite food is pizza,
It is so good to eat,
I love its stringy cheese
Which drips onto my knees
And its crispy base
Has the nicest taste.

Pepperoni, salami, ham, pineapple,
Some of the things you can put on top,
I could eat so much pizza that it would make me go pop!

And if pizza was against the law,
I would have nothing left to gnaw!

Gareth Graham (11)
The Wallace High School

Terrorists

Tall, dark men,
Shooting everywhere trapping everyone,
Creeping around in dark rooms,
When the time comes,
They *pounce!*
And when he takes off his mask,
His face is still covered,
With a beard!
I freeze,
Everything still,
Nothing moving,
Your heart racing,
Short deep breaths,
And then *bang!*
You're dead,
It was all just a dream.

Christopher Cousins (12)
The Wallace High School

Speed

S peed is a weird and wonderful thing.
P eople are sometimes scared of it.
E veryone encounters it sometime in his or her life.
E veryday people are injured by it.
D on't think that you're wise and play with it.

K ill your speed, not a child.
I t kills people if they aren't careful.
L ive as slowly as you can in life.
L eave your life harm free.
S ometimes you cannot handle it.

Matthew Dugan (13)
The Wallace High School

I Dream

I was with my friends
We stopped at the corner candy shop
I had no money except five pence
My friend bought a Dream bar
A lovely, milky, chocolaty Dream bar.

I wanted one so much!
I watched her open the bar,
It crackled as it was opened
I watched her take the first chocolaty bite.

I couldn't resist, I wanted one,
To me it wasn't fair she got one and not me!
I did have money but it was my emergency supply
I guess this was an emergency but still I felt a little guilty
Anyway I took money from it.

I ran all the way back to the candy shop
I bought one, I bought a Dream bar
My Dream bar
I opened the packet it crackled
But this time the crackling belonged to *me*
I took the first dreamy bite.

Heaven!

The sweet, milky chocolate melting slowly in my mouth
And it was my, my sweet, milky chocolate
All mine!

Bethany Downey (12)
The Wallace High School

My Wonderful Treat

As I was doing my homework last night,
A wonderful scent passed my nose.
It smelt like my favourite,
My homework I'll save it until I eat my Swiss roll.

It was smothered in cream and looked like a dream,
Nip me and I shall scream.

With a blink of my eyes,
Such a surprise was laid on the table before me,
It wasn't a dream, the Swiss role with cream,
Was really mine to enjoy.

I chomped and chewed this glorious food,
I'd have some more if I could.
It tasted so sweet,
Oh! What a treat,
It made an electrifying tingle
From my head to my feet.

Julie-Ann Metcalfe (12)
The Wallace High School

Chocolate

My favourite food is chocolate
It's velvety, mouth-watering and creamy.
You can chew it or suck it.
It comes in three different varieties.
White sweet, dark bitter, milk in-between.
My favourite type is milk chocolate.
My favourite brand is Galaxy.
I love using it when I'm cooking.
I love dipping Red Leicester cheese into milk chocolate
When it is melted.

Rebekah Dumican (11)
The Wallace High School

I Hear . . .

When I think of the football pitch I hear . . .

The ref blowing the whistle for the start of the game
Getting beat 2-0, we're doing so lame.
Deadly silence as another flies in
We've pulled a couple back, we might actually win!

Ooh! A crunching tackle on someone in our team
The ref blows his whistle, a penalty, it would seem.
Deep breath as he steps up to take it - *smack!*
In the back of the net, back to 3-3, we're all out of attack.

Thump! From the edge of the box
This could end our rivals mocks,
And it's in - a chorus of cheers
Drinks after the match, the coaches are buying the beers.

Andrew Gilmore (13)
The Wallace High School

The Story Of Chocolate

Chocolate is a wonderful thing
Out of all the sweets, chocolate is the king.
With its creamy centre and smooth outside,
It's the sliding down the highest slide.
So take it solid, take it melted,
You'll want more as soon as you've smelt it.

Chocolate is a thing that comes from Heaven,
I stuff my face full of it, 24/7
If you think I'm not telling the truth
Taste it and you'll go through the roof.

You can get Cadbury's and lots, lots more,
But when I get them they all go into . . .
My chocolate store.

Clark Gibb (11)
The Wallace High School

The Pizza

As we all sit down at the table
The tantalising smell of freshly cooked pizza
Wafts from the kitchen
Onto the table it goes
On a great round dish
Steaming hot.
Next it gets cut into pieces
Sized just right,
I take a slice
And leave it to cool.
When it's sufficiently cool
I take the first bite,
The cheese strings out
Like vines in a jungle
And the pepperoni is lovely and crisp
Like leaves underfoot,
I get to the crust
Which is beautifully crunchy.
Again I take a piece
And it all starts again.

Jed Friskney (11)
The Wallace High School

Strawberries And Cream

I like to have cream with strawberries
All red and juicy and fresh,
And the cream to be whipped and layered
Carefully over my fruit.

I like it when the cream turns pink
From the strawberry juices
And the last thing in the bowl
Is usually some very small strawberry seeds.

Chloe Harris (11)
The Wallace High School

The Ruck

It's cold and the rain is pounding
Mud everywhere and
The grass is slippy.

Scores are equal,
Twenty points each
And we have the ball.

The No 8 makes a ten metre run
He offloads to the out-half,
Who places a cheeky kick
Over the opposition winger.

Our own winger catches it,
Gets tackled and sets the
Muddy ball back.

Next, the scrum half, passes to three
And rampages past the opposing team
Now three draws the full-back,
Passes to the centre and
He scores!

We've won! Full-time whistle
Off we go to shake the disappointed hands
Of the losing team.

Mark Dobbin (12)
The Wallace High School

Snakes

It's coming towards you,
You hear something rustling,
The snake is slithering through the grass,
It stares at you hissing, showing its big fangs,
You freeze as you think about it,
You feel nervous, scared, in case you annoy it,
It slithers past you, the knot in your stomach is unloosened.

Michael Christie (12)
The Wallace High School

Spider

Big, black hairy
Creeping up at me
With its huge fangs
Rearing up to kill.
I'm curled up alone
Waiting in terror
Fear spreading over me.

As it closes in
I couldn't move
With terror,
It was so close
Total darkness.

Was I dead?
No alive, but only just.

Jonathan Crean (12)
The Wallace High School

Wasps

Wasps,
Stripy, black and yellow
Buzzing, stinging, landing
Diving for my food as I freeze with fear!

Wasps,
With spine-shivering stings and eerie eyes
Threatening, creeping, climbing
Striking as soon as they see skin!

Wasps,
Flying, swerving, crawling
Swatting them with newspaper as they enter
My house!
Wasps!

Kathryn Farley (13)
The Wallace High School

Cool, Misty Morning

One cool, misty morning
I went out for a walk
The leaves were rustling wildly
As if each one could talk.

The dew upon the meadow
It scarcely could be seen
For a mist came down so gently
And covered every pasture so green.

It was a lovely morning
There was a gentle breeze
And then the breeze grew stronger
And covered me with leaves.

Grace Timmons (12)
The Wallace High School

Chocolate

Whenever I go to a shop
The voice in my head won't stop
When I eat a chocolate bar
I go to a land quite afar.

Double cream and orange cream
With my taste buds make a team
When I have a double cream

I go to sleep and have a dream

When I'm in bed near my head
A chocolate bar is not too far
If I need food and I'm in the mood
I will have a bite during the night.

Daryl Corbett (11)
The Wallace High School

Dogs

The dangerous red eyes coming towards you,
With pounding paws on the hard black ground.
The leap from the ground as he throws all his weight,
At you.
You are thrown to the ground as it hits your chest,
When a drop of your blood,
Hits him on his chin.
Then as he stands on your chest a drop of pure white saliva
Drools onto your chest
As he bears his white, sharp teeth he catches a sight
A white blur next to the tall, black looming trees.
He gets distracted for a short, split second
And gives you your only chance.
You get up and run but your sudden movement puts him on you
Again.
As you jump the stile in the fence - you think you are safe,
But he jumps it in one go, as if an Olympic medallist jumping
                                                    for its gold.
He backs you against the fence and you know it's all over when,
Bang
It's shot dead on spot in front of you, while you're left thinking,
That could have been me.

Gareth Campbell (12)
The Wallace High School

Gingerbread Men

Warm and pretty staring at me
With liquorice buttons and icing for eyes
Fresh from the oven and beautifully glazed,
Sitting out and waiting to dry.

Time to be eaten, waiting for me,
Sits my gingerbread man patiently,
Then up he jumps, into my arms, I stare at him hungrily,
First it's his head, then it's his legs, before you know it,
He's in my tummy.

Rachel Hynds (11)
The Wallace High School

Sharks

Swimming beyond my line of sight,
Setting up ambushes
Appearing from nowhere as I swim.
Tearing off limbs with ease,
And many razor-sharp teeth.
The ability to eat a person whole,
No chance of escape
As you struggle to swim.
The only safe way to observe or study a shark
Is in a steel cage and wearing chainmail.
Scientists say that sharks are amazing,
Beautiful, interesting creatures.
Regular people say they are 'cool'
But these people don't know what it's like,
They have not had the experience,
I think they are horrifying,
Carnivorous monsters with one instinct,
To eat, eat and eat again,
Until the whole sea is empty.

Adam Ewart (12)
The Wallace High School

Dark

Dark
Black, deep,
No sound,
Just silence,
A creak, I freeze,
Mumbles, groans and sighs,
I listen, no sound,
Just blackness,
I look out the window,
The moon, big, round and bright.
The shadows, the tall shadows,
The tree's long branch, scratching at the window.

Rachael Donaldson (13)
The Wallace High School

Hallowe'en

Like a thunderbolt,
Flashing, exploding in the night sky.
Erupting like an angry volcano!
But then the colours fall like raindrops,
A melting rainbow,
Disappearing all around me!

Little eyes are gazing up
Amazed by the wonderful colours that fill the sky!
Dressed in black, green, purple!
Ah! What scary faces they have!
But now the little children are staring into the big, roaring
Flames!
Their sticky, toffee apples are melting, running as they are
Beside the red-hot fire!
Their happy faces tell it all,
They are enjoying this wonderful scene!

Rat-a-tat-tat, trick or treaters are knocking on doors,
Hoping for a sweet, a penny?
But the hours are ticking by, and little eyes are tried and
Sleepy,
Climbing up the carpeted stairs,
Sleeping . . . sleeping . . . zzzzzzzz

Jade Drury (13)
The Wallace High School

Lettuce

I love lettuce
The crunchy, crispy kind
The way it tastes in your mouth is refreshing,
It feels like plastic in your mouth but tasty all the same,
Perhaps in an iceburg lettuce pasta salad
You might discover it,
Vinegar adds a slight bitterness along with a sweet sensation,
When it's ice-cold it tastes the best,
So that's why I love lettuce above the rest!

Leah Hammond (11)
The Wallace High School

Machine Babies

Babies are the machines,
They cry,
Then sleep,
Then cry,
Then sleep.
Sometimes you wish they never cried,
Or never did anything bad,
But what if they didn't?
They wouldn't be babies at all,
They would be broken down machines.

Babies are like machines,
You push a wrong button,
Or pull a wrong cord,
They go out of control like machines
You can't stop them or do anything,
They just cry,
And cry,
And cry.
They will not stop until they have a dummy,
Just like pulling the plug on a machine.

Babies are like machines.

Nathan Dickson (12)
The Wallace High School

My Favourite Sweet

My favourite sweet is a sherbet lemon
The way it fizzes on your tongue
It's tangy, fizzy taste
I'd like to open the wrapper
And put the sweet into my mouth.
I like to open the packet of sweets on my suite.
I like to sit at night watching the television eating them.
It feels hard against my teeth like a stone on the street
And that's what I think of my lemon, fizzy sweet.

Stewart Evans (11)
The Wallace High School

Pumpkin

What's inside the pumpkin?

Chanting of children,
Running to different doors,
Screeches of laughter.

Yellow cats' eyes
Black fur and scraping claws,
Jumping on their prey.

Howling upon the moon,
Scuffling and yapping noises,
Hunting at night.

Skeletons at the graveyard
Zombies shuffling and hopping without a foot,
Rising from their grave.

Cackling from above
Witches flying on broomsticks.
Warts on their noses,
Wearing black capes,
Long, green fingers reaching out.

Bright eyes, candle wax,
Lids toppling over, candles going out,
Sweets all around, it's Hallowe'en night!

Kathryn Dowse (12)
The Wallace High School

Planes

Unpredictable, metallic,
Flying, turning, drifting,
Experiences some unexpected turbulence,
I'm rocked in my seat,
A woman screams and panic arises,
Flight attendants rush down the aisle,
They show signs of fear,
But the plane floats on.

The captain's voice fills the plane,
Tries to assure that nothing's wrong,
But in fact there is,
I can feel it.

Suddenly the oxygen masks come down
Nausea fills my lungs,
I can barely breathe,
Lifejackets are ripped from under seats,
The room is spinning,
My stomach churns,
This is it,
We're going down,
What can I do?
Nothing . . .

The impact's immense,
I'm launched back in my seat,
Still . . . stillness . . . sick stillness . . .
Black . . . blackness . . . barbaric blackness.

Jamie Clements (13)
The Wallace High School

Jack Frost

Creaking the old house stands
Rubbing together my hands
As Jack Frost comes creeping in
Creeping in
Creeping in.

With moonlight shining silver
And stars twinkling forever
He's seen cold crisp on the ground
Crisp on the ground
Crisp on the ground.
Brrr!

As it gets dark
You'll hear the old dog bark
And then silence.

Goodnight . . . Jack Frost.

Pamela McClure (11)
The Wallace High School

Spiders

Hairy, deadly, black, sleek bodies
Scuttling and scurrying all over my room
Mounded upon a weaved web
It drops spindling from the roof
It descends with great pace
Getting closer, closer, closer
Finally it stops
I can see its black beady eyes
I can see its deadly sting coming down
Then in one death defying climax
It drops!
Spiders.

Jonathan Dunn (13)
The Wallace High School

Call From Aisling?

Insides freeze
Heart as still as stone
Pick up the phone
Pick up the phone.

Could it be her?
I don't know
It's a dangerous hope
But a hope all the same
Pick up the phone,
Pick up the phone.

Stare at the phone
Could it be my dark-haired sister?
Brown-eyed girl in a far away land?
I wish I could know
But there's only one way
Pick up the phone
Pick up the phone.

Sukie McFarland (11)
The Wallace High School

Food In General

Strawberries soaked in sugar
Glistening in juice
Light and fluffy chocolate mousse.

Freshly baked pizza with
Crispy chips,
Garlic bread with garlic butter
Dripping down my lips.

Smooth and creamy
Chocolate sauce,
Crunchy salad all mixed and tossed.

Now I eat the gooey trifle,
And go to the fridge for another rifle.

Naomi Fleming (11)
The Wallace High School

Insects!

Different colours, spotted, striped, creeping,
Crawling, and biting.

- insects, nipping, egg laying, web making and
with those eerie eyes, hard bodied, soft bodied,
individual in their own creepy ways.

- insects, hiding in the soil, or hiding in the night,
squishing under my shoe - yuk!

Insects! Insects! Insects!

- sometimes they fly and land or crawl up your leg!
One of the things I hate most in my life is,

Insects!

Devon Crossley (12)
The Wallace High School

Chocolate

Oh chocolate, how can I live without it,
Slowly it vanishes bit by bit.
My mouth waters with the lovely smell,
With my favourite fillings honeycomb, mint chips
And caramel.

When I grow up my dream job to be,
A chocolate tester at Cadbury's, all the chocolate for me.

Chomping it in a minute,
Dipping it in tea,
Spreading it on toast,
I always make the most of all the chocolate
I see.

Sarah Geddis (12)
The Wallace High School

Fun For Some - Fear For Others!

Roller coasters! Those dreaded words.
The chatter of excited people queuing up.
Waiting, tense, whilst I tremble in fear.
My legs, limbs and arms have frozen like ice;
An ice statue surrounded by crowds.
The whirlwind of screams from children.
I look at the curly wurly roller coaster spiralling
Up and down, up and down, round and round.
The queue gets shorter and shorter and so does the time.
My heart is in my mouth,
As I move to the front of the crowds.
I am breaking out in a cold sweat.
I can't speak, can't breathe, can't move.
The ride stops, people shoving, pushing to get off.
They sway and swagger like drunk men,
Clutching their heads in agony.
I stagger forward and trip as I miss the step up;
Too fixated on other matters.
I stumble forward and sit into the seat.
The bars are secured around me.
It feels like being trapped in a cage - no way out!
Squeezing my eyes tightly shut,
I feel the ride vibrate.
Higher and higher it goes.
I can see only darkness.
Like a blind man, suddenly I am jolted forward,
Down, down into the nightmare!

Laura Donaldson (12)
The Wallace High School

Pavlova

And there it was sitting there,
A dessert among all desserts
I came nearer, nearer, nearer
It sang out to me as if
It was waiting for me.

Somebody lifts a piece
I start to panic
Another piece goes
I start to run like a manic
I dive, I jump.

Noooooooo!

I get it!
Extreme bliss, fruit and fresh cream
With a sticky centre.
It took a while
To get it but it
Didn't last long where it was going,
But it was worth every bit.

So ever since then
I have reserved a bit
And ever since then I have said

It was worth it!

Jonathan Grattan (11)
The Wallace High School

Oh Sweetie Shop

Oh sweetie shop
Oh sweetie shop
I stand there, watch in awe
The jars of magic, sealed behind
The glorious, big red door.

The bell it rings
The sound so dear
I've made my entrance
Shopkeeper appear.

The colours change
Smooth ball on my tongue
Gobstoppers so big
They live so long.

Zebra sweets
I called them so
Freshness of mint
Could I say no?

A sherbet surprise
A crunchy lemon case
Stick to my teeth
It was worth, for the taste.

Oh sweetie shop
Oh sweetie shop
I stood here, watched in awe
For I am old and teeth have gone
How I wish I was back aged four.

Emily Gardner (12)
The Wallace High School

Brussels Sprouts

The Brussels sprout is green
The most revolting taste there's been
They look like a small cabbage
They taste worse than old garbage
They are small and round
They grow out of the ground
If you eat one you deserve a pound.

My mum serves them on a plate
She thinks they are great
When I see them in the shop
I ask my mum not to stop
When she puts them on to boil
My stomach starts to coil
I'd like to throw them in the River Foyle.

Nicholas Freeburn (11)
The Wallace High School

Chocolate

Box on the table full of chocolate
Milk chocolate, dark chocolate
What one will I chomp on?
Hand creeping slowly shuffling round the box
Mouth-watering wildly
Hand sweating terribly
I didn't eat milk
I didn't eat dark
But I ate both.

Craig Lowry (12)
The Wallace High School

Pizza

Watch the dough go up in the air
Spinning around without a care.
He puts the tomato on the top
And then the cheese which will sizzle and pop.

On goes the salami and chicken too
Other toppings it's up to you.
In the oven to harden up
In twenty minutes the time will be up.

When it comes out the smell is great
And when it's done we're in a state.

Richard Graham (12)
The Wallace High School

Sweet Problem

Walking about along the street,
I was looking for something to eat.
I was out of money, the shops were closed,
So out on the street, there I nosed
For something to eat,
Until I saw a small brown sweet
Covered it was
In bits and bobs,
With lots of fluff and other stuff.
A quick rub with my hand and the sweet was grand.
Straight onto my tongue,
Yum, yum, yum!

Jennifer Gilpin (12)
The Wallace High School